Green Fund Book No. 19

The Union of Christian Forces in America

BY

ROBERT A. ASHWORTH, D. D.

PASTOR OF THE FIRST BAPTIST CHURCH, MILWAUKEE, WIS.; MEMBER
OF THE EXECUTIVE COMMITTEE OF THE FEDERAL COUNCIL OF CHURCHES
OF CHRIST IN AMERICA

A PRIZE BOOK

PHILADELPHIA
AMERICAN SUNDAY-SCHOOL UNION
1816 Chestnut Street

Copyright, 1915, by the
AMERICAN SUNDAY-SCHOOL UNION

PUBLISHER'S NOTE

THIS book is issued by the American Sunday-School Union under the John C. Green Income Fund. It won the prize of $1000 in a competition for the best manuscript on the subject of CHRISTIAN UNITY. The provisions of the fund authorize the Union to choose the subject,—which must always be germane to the object of the Society,—and to control the copyright, thus reducing the price of the book. In this way works of a high order of merit may be put into circulation at a reasonable price. The author is given large liberty in the literary form, style, and treatment of the subject.

The book treats a theme which is at present of universal interest throughout Christendom. That it was the prize-winner in a competition in which many able and scholarly manuscripts were submitted is a sufficient proof of its exceptional merit. The author has served as President of the Federation of Churches in his own city, and now represents his denomination on the Executive Committee of the Federal Council of Churches of Christ in America.

He approaches his subject, therefore, not merely as an interested observer and student of conditions of church life in America to-day, but as a leader in the movement to harmonize differences and promote unity through mutual understanding, sympathy, and co-operation. His book is a valuable contribution toward solving the problem and furthering the movement which it treats.

PREFACE

THIS book is the expression of the writer's very earnest conviction that for the present no progress will be made in the direction of Christian Unity by a discussion of denominational differences, but that the need of the hour is a fuller development of that co-operation in practical tasks which is already possible among Christian bodies, despite doctrinal or other disagreements. Such co-operation will promote mutual acquaintance and esteem, and these in turn will evoke Christian love; and if love, when it is perfected, cannot draw Christians together into the unity of a single Church, it is hopeless to expect that any other motive whatsoever will suffice to do it. Thus the most hopeful program for the present is co-operation in common tasks; then federation; to be followed, if it be God's will, by organic unity. The process cannot be hurried, neither can the order of the steps in it be reversed. This is the era of federation. Until the possibilities of the federative principle are thoroughly tested, and the spirit of it thoroughly permeates the divided bodies of Christendom, no further step can be taken.

The author desires to express his very hearty appreciation of the assistance rendered by his friends, the Rev. F. W. C. Meyer and Mr. H. C. Henderson; also by Rev. James McConaughy, Editor of Publications of the American Sunday-School Union, after the acceptance of the manuscript. Their examination of it led to many helpful suggestions. He sends forth this book with the earnest prayer that it may make some slight contribution toward the consummation of that unity of the Church for which the Lord of all Christians prayed.

ROBERT A. ASHWORTH.

CONTENTS

Neither for these only do I pray, but for them also that believe on me through their word; that they may all be one; even as thou, Father, art in me, and I in thee, that they also may be in us: that the world may believe that thou didst send me. And the glory which thou hast given me I have given unto them; that they may be one, even as we are one; I in them, and thou in me, that they may be perfected into one; that the world may know that thou didst send me, and lovedst them, even as thou lovedst me.
—John 17:20–23, R. V.

THE EXPENSE AND WASTE OF
CHRISTIAN DISUNION

Protestantism divided and subdivided.—The multiplicity of denominations.—Its effect in loss of spiritual fellowship.—An equal loss in efficiency.—Over-churching and its effects in waste of equipment and unnecessary expense of maintenance. —The inadequate salaries of ministers.—Loss in prestige and leadership.—A divided Church unable to render the service to be expected from it.

THE UNION OF CHRISTIAN
FORCES IN AMERICA

CHAPTER I

THE EXPENSE AND WASTE OF CHRISTIAN DISUNION

THE most pressing problem of the Church in our day is that of Christian Unity: beside it all others fade into insignificance. The energies of Christendom are being frittered away in the competitions, controversies, jealousies, and friction engendered by its "unhappy divisions," and this in the face of such demands upon the Church and such opportunities for service as have never been presented before in its history. This era, that might be the most glorious in the career of the Church, may be compelled to record the story of its degeneration and defeat. The loss of influence that institutional Christianity is suffering to-day may be ascribed to many causes, but to none is it due in so large a measure as to disunion. The most difficult situations which the Church is called upon to meet, it has itself created: its worst enemies are of its own household. There is no task confronting it anywhere in the world which the Church might not accomplish if it could approach that task with a united front; and there is none to which it is fully equal so long as its forces are divided and its energies dissipated.

The first step in a constructive program for the reunion of Christendom is the frank recognition of the lengths to which the multiplication of sects has gone, and of the serious evils that flow therefrom. It is a futile waste of time to try to fix the blame for the existing situation. "Protestantism," Dr. James H. Ecob once said, "is divided and subdivided until it cannot count its own *disjecta membra*. This condition should be taken upon the conscience and heart of every serious man and woman as a burden and a shame." Another has declared that the divisions of Christendom might be classified into "sects and insects." But whatever truth there may be in such statements, sectarianism will never be scolded or ridiculed out of existence. It was not mere perversity that called any one of the denominations into being. Every denomination sincerely believes itself to have a right to be and to propagate its principles, even though to it every other may seem to be without excuse. The mistakes of the fathers were honestly made; and if we have a wider vision than they and are ready now to move out of the "low-vaulted past" and to set our hands to the building of a loftier temple, little is to be gained by stopping to rake over the ashes of dead controversies to discover how the foundations of earlier structures were laid. We may be quite willing to admit that the sectarian spirit has rendered valuable service to the cause of the Kingdom in the past, and yet be thoroughly convinced that its days of vigor and usefulness are gone and that it is ready for the grave, and that denominationalism, as we know it, must be radically transformed if it is to meet the demands of the present day.

Knowledge of religious conditions existing in America to-day must convince even the firmest advocate of individualism and independence in religion that they have exceeded the bounds of liberty. Those who desire the statistics may consult the authoritative work of Dr. H. K. Carroll, *The Religious Forces of the United States*.[1]

"The first impression one gets in studying the results of the census," says Dr. Carroll, "is that there is an infinite variety of religions in the United States. There are churches small and churches great, churches white and churches black, churches high and low, orthodox and heterodox, Christian and pagan, Catholic and Protestant, Liberal and

[1] P. xiii ff.

Conservative, Calvinistic and Arminian, native and foreign, Trinitarian and Unitarian. All phases of thought are represented by them, all possible theologies, all varieties of polity, ritual, usage, forms of worship. . . . This we speak of as 'the land of the free.' No man has a property in any other man, or a right to dictate his religious principles or denominational attachment. No church has a claim on the State, and the State has no claim on any church. We scarcely appreciate our advantages. Our citizens are free to choose a residence in any one of 50 states and territories, and to move from one to another as often as they have a mind to. There is even a wider range for choice and change in religion. One may be a pagan, a Jew, or a Christian, or each in turn. If he is a pagan, he may worship in one of the numerous temples devoted to Buddha; if a Jew, he may be of the Orthodox or Reformed variety; if a Christian, he may select any one of 125 or 130 different kinds, or join every one of them in turn. He may be six kinds of an Adventist, seven kinds of a Catholic, twelve kinds of a Mennonite or Presbyterian, thirteen kinds of a Baptist, sixteen kinds of a Lutheran, or seventeen kinds of a Methodist. He may be a member of any one of 143 denominations, or of all in succession. If none of these suits him, he still has a choice among 150 separate and independent congregations, which have no denominational name, creed, or connection."

It affords a degree of comfort, however, to be assured that these rainbow-hued varieties of Christian practice may be reduced by a process of synthesis to a more manageable number. "A closer scrutiny of the list shows that many of these 143 denominations differ only in name. Without a single change in doctrine or polity, the 18 Methodist bodies could be reduced to three or four; the 12 Presbyterian to three; the 12 Mennonite to two; and so on. The differences in many cases are only sectional or historical. The slavery question was the cause of not a few divisions, and matters of discipline were responsible for a larger number. Arranging the denominations in groups or families, and counting as one family each of the 12 Mennonite, the 17 Methodist, the 13 Baptist bodies, and so on, we have, instead of 143, only 42 titles. In other words, if there could be a consolidation of each denominational group, the reproach of our division would be largely taken away."[1]

That the splintering process from which the cause of religion has suffered has not altogether ceased is indicated in the bulletin of the Department of Commerce and Labor of figures gathered in 1906, which reports that during the sixteen years subsequent to

[1] Dr. H. K. Carroll, *The Religious Forces of the United States*, p. xv.

2

the census of 1890, 41 new divisions were added to
the unhappy list. There is, however, here also a
gleam of comfort in that many of these are not
Christian, and others can hardly be called churches,
so small are they and insignificant.

The facts, however interpreted, are serious
enough. There is no single characteristic of organized Christianity which has not served as a cause of
division. In polity the churches are known as congregational, presbyterial, and episcopal. The question of ministerial orders has been a fruitful cause
of division. The Roman Catholic Church admits
the validity of the orders of the Greek Orthodox
Church, but there is no fellowship between them.
The Roman Catholic and Greek Orthodox Churches
unite in denying validity to the orders of the Anglican and Protestant Episcopal Churches, while the
latter refuse to recognize the orders of any
churches except those that refuse to recognize theirs.
Churches divide on the observance of ritual and on
the manner of observance and significance of the
ordinances. It is among the ironies of history that
the ordinance of the Supper of our Lord, wherein
it was intended that disciples should manifest their
unity about a common table, has been a principal
occasion and cause of division.

Should other sources of disagreement fail, there
remain dogma and creed which may safely be de-

pended upon to keep the followers of Jesus apart.
It would be instructive to count the separate doctrines that are to be found in the creeds of Christendom, and to point out the manner in which the
simple truths of the apostolic Church have taken on
complexity with the years, and to note how, with
every advance in the intricacy of belief, there has
been a further scattering of believers. A few years
ago there appeared a dispatch from Peru, announc-
ing that the traditional treasure of the Incas, a
sum of vast amount, had been discovered at Challa-
catta. The item concluded with the statement,
"The discoverers are now quarreling over the
treasure." Thus has the company of the disciples
of our Lord been prevented from applying the wealth
of the gospel to the needs of man by their disputes
over its possession and administration.

For the disunion that has characterized the history of Protestantism we are paying the penalty,—
a penalty so severe that it threatens to bankrupt
the resources of the Church. As a consequence
of such disunion, organized Christianity has suffered irreparably, in the first place, from *the loss of
spiritual fellowship*. There is much that the
churches could learn from one another if they
would. Every great denomination that has given
proof of its endurance, and that has gathered into
its fold large numbers of people, must have its pecu-

liar virtues. If it has been able to minister to the spiritual needs of the multitude of its adherents, it must possess spiritual vitality and at least a modicum of spiritual truth. One does not gather figs of thistles. It is impossible to believe that God could so largely use any body of believers as he has used each of the several churches that make up the bulk of Christendom if it were devoid of any essential element of divine truth. Yet there is no church among them all but has its failings, none without its alloy of error, not one but that is impeded by a partial view of truth. Where one is strong, another is weak; where one fails, another succeeds.

It has been often said that denominational differences are temperamental, and that the various Christian bodies appeal to various types of men, their members being drawn to one another by a "consciousness of kind." If this be true in any degree, what is it but a confession of the partiality and bias of every such communion, and of the inability of any one of them to appeal to all sorts and conditions of men? But if that be true, does it not prove that no existing church reflects the full-orbed Christ, but only a fraction of his refulgence? Christ is "divided" among them. There is no church that sees more than a single facet of the jewel, not one but that is blind to the full glory of the revelation. For Christ himself appeals to every tem-

perament and to the entire man, and the richer the
man's personality, the more complete his development, the more rounded his character, the stronger
the appeal. And if the appeal of the Church to the
world is to be a universal appeal, attracting every
type of man and revealing the complete Christ to
the entire man, the fractional revelations of particular churches must be united. No one can fully
understand Christ except in the fellowship of all
kinds of believers. They who approach him from
varied angles must bring their contributions to the
common store, if the Church's conception of the
Christ is to be rich enough and full enough to win
the world. Some see the breadth, and some the
length, and others the depth, and still others the
height; but if the Christian is ever to "be able to
comprehend what is the breadth *and* length *and*
depth *and* height, and to know the love of Christ,
which passeth knowledge," and thus "be filled with
all the fulness of God," it must be "with *all* the
saints." No man or church, in our divided state,
is large enough to comprehend this alone, and that
is why our views are still prejudiced and partial
and devoid of compelling power. If we are to understand the Christ, we must come to him together.
Paul desired to visit the brethren in Rome that he
might impart unto them "some spiritual gift";—
that is, that he might share with them the product

of an experience of the Christ that they did not possess;—but he desired also to gain from them, for the strengthening and broadening of his own spiritual life, that which they had gained from another angle,—"that I with you may be comforted in you, each of us by the other's faith, both yours and mine."

The separate companies of the disciples of the Lord, therefore, have suffered irreparable damage through their long estrangement, in being deprived of that mutual enlargement that springs from spiritual fellowship. We are shut off from one another by denominational fences sometimes so high that we cannot see over them. Here are churches that lack the historic sense. They are but of yesterday, and have never experienced the charm or felt the conserving influence of Christian tradition; but they are moving vigorously forward with power under the influence of a mighty passion for the living Christ. Here, on the other hand, are churches adorned with the gifts of the centuries. They are like vases set in some cathedral at Easter time into which the worshipers, as they pass, drop rich garments and jewels. But they are burdened by the very wealth of their heritage, and the dignity of their ritual hampers the spirit. They lack freedom and spontaneity. Here are churches strong in doctrine: out of them have come the great theologians and teachers of Christendom. Here are others with a more popular and democratic appeal, who know better how to gain and keep the ear of the common people. Cannot the denominations learn from one another and share their gifts? The weakness of the witness of the Church lies in its disunion. Only a united Church can understand or reveal the Lord of the Church. It takes all the seven colors of the spectrum to make the sunlight: the sun cannot express itself through a single color. Nor can the Christ express himself through a broken fragment of his body, the Church: therefore he prayed, "That they may all be one, as thou, Father, art in me, and I in thee; that the world may believe that thou didst send me."

In a little book entitled *In Praise of Legend*, there is told the story of "a people living in a world which is divided into three countries, Cerulia, Rubia, and Flavia. Parsee-like, they worship the Sun. None could see the Sun itself, but each worshiped through the peculiar color seen as through a prism by each—blue, red, or yellow. Each believed his own color to be the only color of the Deity:

> 'Cerulians see all things blue;
> Through red the Rubians all view;
> While Flavians indeed declare
> There's naught but yellow in the air.'

Each country holds that none can approach the Sun—

> 'Except along the path of light
> Which each declares alone is right.'

And so each despises the other. . . . So they live their lives, each tenacious of his own creed, and all full of contempt for those who differ from them. At length one day a sage appears among them and tries to put them right.   He tells them:

> 'The Light
> Which after death will meet their sight,
> Will not be yellow, blue, or red,
> But white and glorious instead,
> A pure and everlasting blaze
> Of beautiful, love-blended rays.'

The lesson is," the author continues, "that Truth is only seen through prisms by the unit.   Not until each sees the truth as seen by the whole will each grasp the fact that his own color is only one hue in it, and must blend with the other colors before it can be called *the* Truth.   Each has his own quota to contribute and each will see more as he tries to see through the eyes of all.   It is only the whole Church that can see the whole Truth."

Upon *the administrative side of its activity* also the Church has suffered a disastrous loss of efficiency through its divisions.   This is evident in many quarters in the prevalence, to use an odious but seemingly indispensable term, of "over-churching." There will be differences of opinion as to the degree of its prevalence, and as to the point at which it makes its appearance, but no disagreement as to its existence.

From a study of the statistics of 1910, as given by Dr. Carroll, of the following larger divisions of Protestants within the United States, Baptists (Regular, North and South, and Free), Congregationalists, Disciples, Methodists (North and South), Presbyterians (North and South), and Protestant Episcopalians, it appears that in these bodies are 13,385,600 communicants, with 76,783 ministers and 116,012 edifices. From the statistics of the Roman Catholic Church of the same date it appears that for 12,425,947 communicants there are 17,084 priests and 13,461 churches. Thus for the Protestant denominations mentioned there was a church building to every 115 communicants, and a minister to every 173 communicants, while for the Roman Catholic Church there was a church building for every 923 communicants, and one priest, on the average, for 727 communicants. If we deduct 20 per cent. from the number of Protestant ministers, and 10 per cent. from the number of Roman Catholic priests, which have been suggested on plausible grounds as the proper percentages[1]

[1] Rev. F. Marion Simms, *What Must the Church Do to be Saved?* p. 77 ff.

to include those who are superannuated, engaged in secretarial work, or as foreign missionaries, it would provide a Protestant minister to every 218 communicants, and a Roman Catholic priest to every 809 communicants. On the basis of the figures for all denominations for 1906, which is the latest date for which complete statistics are available, the Rev. F. Marion Simms asserts that we had, at that date, "one active Protestant pastor in the United States for every 173 Protestant church members, which is one for every 597 non-Catholic population;" while, "on the average, each priest in the United States in 1906 cared for 1,040 souls."[1]

The Rev. E. Tallmadge Root, on the basis of the 1906 census, declares that "for the United States, Protestants provide 53,282,445 sittings for 20,287,742 communicants: so that if the maximum attendance equals the membership, which is not probable, they have two and one-half times as many sittings as are ever used; while the Catholics provide only 4,494,377 sittings for 12,079,142 communicants, almost exactly reversing the ratio of sittings and communicants." After all allowances are made for differences in the modes and conceptions of worship which distinguish Catholics from Protestants, and which permit the former to care for a larger number of worshipers in a single building than is possible to

[1] Rev. F. Marion Simms, *What Must the Church Do to be Saved?*

the latter, there is still reason to ask, with Mr. Root, whether it would not seem that Protestants are bearing a far larger burden in the maintenance of church equipment than should be necessary. Says the Rev. E. T. Tomlinson, "A careful study of the data presented (for the United States) shows that there are 192,795 church edifices (Protestant) with an average of 157 members per organization, and that the debt of the average body is nearly 50 per cent. of the value of the church property. This implies a heavy tax on the membership even before its legitimate work is begun. With a membership of 157, it is estimated that at least two-thirds of the membership are women. This leaves 52 male members, of whom doubtless a large proportion are boys too young to be of much financial assistance. If only one-third is deducted for non-resident members, there are left approximately 20 to 30 men upon whom must fall the chief burden of support of the 'average' church. What such a tax would be if raised for other than church purposes is apparent."[1] An experienced Christian worker has stated it to be his opinion that any community can support a church to every 500 of the population; but the question at issue is not how small a number of people may conceivably maintain a church, but

[1] Rev. E. T. Tomlinson, Ph. D., "Too Many Churches," in *The World's Work*, August, 1913.

how large a population may be efficiently served by a single church and a single minister.

The penalty of the crowding of churches into one community is commonly the neglect of other and neighboring communities. During the last two or three years the Board of Home Missions of the Presbyterian Church (North), under the direction of its Department of Church and Country Life, has made extensive surveys of various parts of the country, from which interesting information as to the relation of the number of churches to the population may be gleaned. In Illinois the 44 communities investigated, which included rural districts and towns up to a population of 3,000 and a total population of 114,975, contained 225 churches, in which 20 different denominations were represented,—an average of five churches to the community. Only 77 of these churches had grown in ten years. Forty-seven churches, abandoned during that period, were still standing, while many others had been torn down. Only 19 per cent. of the population attended church regularly and 50 per cent. of the Protestant membership did not attend. There was one church to every 511 of the population, with an average attendance of 93. Meanwhile, there were 30 rural communities without a church within a radius of five miles, leaving 48 per cent. of the population absolutely untouched by the Church.   In Pennsylvania 53 communities, with a population of 124,203, were studied, within which were 348 churches, or one to every 357 people. Forty-two per cent. of the population were church members, of whom 69 per cent. attended regularly, the church-goers constituting 29 per cent. of the population. Fifty per cent. of the churches were growing, 26 per cent. standing still, and 24 per cent. declining. Five communities were without a church within a radius of five miles. In Missouri there were found in 23 villages, averaging 240 in population, 56 churches, or one to every 100 people. Four villages had four churches each, and two of these villages had less than 225 inhabitants each. The surveys in Ohio and Indiana give results of a similar character.

NOTE.—Dr. Tomlinson, in the article quoted above, gives the following statistics for Vermont:

	Population.	Number of Churches.
Bennington	6,000	6
Brandon	2,000	5
Castleton	1,000	4
Center Rutland	200	1
East Hubbardton	470	2
East Poultney	300	2
Fair Haven	3,500	8
Fowler	200	1
Hydeville	150	2
Ira	600	1
Manchester	2,200	5
Mendon	200	2
Middletown Springs	150	1
North Bennington	800	3
Pittsford	425	5

	Population.	Number of Churches.
Poultney	2,500	5
Pownal	150	2
Proctor	1,200	3
Rutland	13,500	14
Shaftesbury	500	3
Wallingford	700	3
West Haven	300	2
West Pawlet	500	3
West Rutland	4,500	11

This is an average of a church to about 447 people. One county in the state of Massachusetts contains a church for every 295 inhabitants. In Webster County, Kentucky, are 68 Protestant churches, one to every 308 of the population, with an average membership of less than 90.

Conditions such as these, examples of which might be furnished almost indefinitely from every section of the country, effectually dispose of the question whether over-churching exists. If further illustrations are desired, they may be obtained in the results of the intensive studies of Tompkins county, New York, and Windsor county, Vermont, by C. O. Gill and Gifford Pinchot, published in a volume entitled *The Country Church*. These studies tell the same story of the reduplication of churches, with the heavy burden of expense and loss of efficiency and the decreasing membership and attendance that go with it. Nor are these conditions confined to village and country communities. The cities suffer from them also, as many authorities agree.

The present generation is not so largely to blame for the disabilities under which it labors as are generations past, that, in a day when denominational feeling ran higher than now, felt driven to further their sectarian propaganda by the founding of churches wherever they could secure a foothold. But in very many communities the sour grapes of the fathers have set the children's teeth on edge. The children wrestle with problems which they should never have been called upon to face. In addition to the natural and inevitable difficulties of Christian work, especially in small communities, they must struggle with artificial hindrances set for them by the unwise zeal of their predecessors.

The consequence of the unbearable expense of maintenance, where churches are multiplied beyond the ability of communities adequately to sustain them, falls most heavily upon the ministry in the inadequacy of salaries. It is unfair to the many noble men who labor in such communities, in many instances with a rare degree of self-sacrifice, to require them to expend their energies under the discouragement that comes from the suspicion or certainty that, because of the multiplication of churches, their efforts are not needed. But when such men, many of them with a training that has cost much in money and in time, are asked to toil for the wage of unskilled labor, it becomes a crime against the spirit of religion.

The average salary of ministers of all denominations in the United States was stated by the census

report of 1906, the latest figures available, to be
$663, or an average of $12.75 per week; and the average for all denominations in communities outside
the principal cities was reported to be $573, or $11.02
per week.   Though the minister must be thoroughly
and expensively trained, and is put to great expense
to maintain his efficiency, his average wage is thus
seen to be far below the level of the average paid to
the mechanic.   Taking for comparison the figures
for the same year presented by the Bureau of Labor
we find the following to have been the average wages
paid at that date in the occupations named: brick-
layers, $29.05 per week; carpenters, $15.46; plas-
terers, $27.82; glass-blowers (window glass), $38.29;
compositors, $18.87; and cigar-makers, $17.42.[1]

[1] *Bulletin of the Bureau of Labor*, No. 71, 1907.

The following are the figures from the census of 1906 that indicate
the actual average salaries paid by the principal Protestant denominations in the United States in communities of less than 25,000 population:

Southern Baptist Convention	$334
Disciples or Christians	526
United Brethren	547
Methodist Episcopal (South)	681
Northern Baptist Convention	683
Methodist Episcopal (North)	741
Lutheran	744
Presbyterian Church in the U. S. (South)	857
Congregational	880
Reformed Church in America	923
Presbyterian Church in the U. S. A. (North)	977
Universalists	987
Protestant Episcopal	994

These figures should be interpreted in terms of the cost of living, which
varies in different sections of the country.

It seems probable, further, that the salaries of ministers, especially in rural communities, are growing smaller rather than larger. In the study of Windsor and Tompkins counties, already referred to, the authors say, "The churches of both counties are giving less and less pay to their ministers. Reckoned in dollars, there was an increase of 16 per cent. in Windsor county, while in Tompkins county the increase was less than one per cent. Reckoned in purchasing power, less real pay was given in each county during the second period than in the first (*i. e.*, twenty years earlier). The amount of real pay declined seven per cent. in Windsor county and nearly 16 per cent. in Tompkins county."[1]

Such salaries where they are insufficient to sustain their recipients at even a low degree of efficiency must be eked out with aid from state and national missionary boards, a large fraction of whose funds must go to the support of churches engaged in competitive and often superfluous activity. Meanwhile great districts within the United States are without a church or religious privileges of any kind, and while the religious interests of many communities in the home land are actually depressed by a surplus of churches and ministers, the forces at work upon the foreign field cry for reinforcements.

These evils of over-churching, and consequent

[1] *Loco. cit.*, p. 14.

3

loss of spiritual fellowship between the various bodies of Christians who are forced into competition with one another, together with this waste of equipment and unnecessary expense of church maintenance, and handicapping of ministers through the payment of inadequate salaries, are a part of the price that Protestantism is paying for the luxury of its divisions. But these do not constitute the entire cost. There results from the disunion of Protestantism an incalculable loss in national and local prestige and leadership.

The usefulness of the Church in the local community is sadly impaired by this division of its forces. There is no argument for Christianity like the unity of Christians. When the voices of all the churches blend in a single message there is weight and power behind it. Competition between churches that claim to be servants of the same Master seems to the world so incongruous with the spirit of that Master as to impair the credentials of the institution that professes to represent him.

In its divided state the Church is unable to render to the nation the service which is rightfully expected of it. The State has relieved the Church of the burdens of taxation and accorded to it a place of special privilege with the expectation of certain services in return. The Church ought to be the incarnate conscience of the State. In the midst of

the starving, hurried, restless populace, bent upon
gain and power, it stands with spire pointing to the
skies, a perpetual witness to truths whose values are
eternal. It is the task of the Church to spiritualize
the ideals of democracy; but from its often discordant and always divided witness what unity of
impression upon the national life is possible? In
the danger of a loss of influence that shall be complete and final the perils of disunion reach their cul-
mination. All systematic religious education has
been crowded out of the public schools, to their immeasurable loss and peril, largely because the
churches cannot agree upon what teaching shall be
furnished. The Church is losing its authority over
family life. An increasing proportion of marriage
ceremonies are performed by officers of the State
without the sanction of religion, and the percentage
of divorces advances rapidly. Large areas of thought
have been permitted to pass beyond the controlling
influence of the Church, and an increasing percentage
of religious feeling and activity is to be found outside of, and out of relation to it. Thus irreligion
feeds upon the follies of the representatives of
religion. The organized efforts for human betterment, whose passion has stirred our legislatures and
courts of justice and commercial institutions, this
new "enthusiasm of humanity" that has come upon
the world in our day, is not led by the Church. Too

often the Church is found near the rear of the procession, swept into it by the suction of the mighty movement as the army of progress marches by. Why does not the Church lead? Because it is paralyzed by its divisions, like a body in which a nerve is. cut, so that the members have lost their connection with each other and with the organizing brain, and cannot move together. There is danger that the Church will lose not only the place of leadership, but the capacity for it as well, unless it shall learn again, like the church at Philippi, how to "stand fast in one spirit, with one mind, striving together for the faith of the gospel."

THE NEW TESTAMENT IDEAL OF
CHRISTIAN UNITY AND
WHAT BECAME OF IT

The unity taught by Christ—a unity of spirit; a moral unity; a vital unity.—Unity of the apostolic churches.—Teaching of Paul upon the subject.—Unity by coercion in the Roman Church.—Effect of the Reformation.—Present conditions and agencies in America conducive to Christian unity.

CHAPTER II

THE NEW TESTAMENT IDEAL OF CHRISTIAN UNITY AND WHAT BECAME OF IT

IT is among the most hopeful signs of our times that Christians within every communion are coming to realize how serious and wicked a thing it is that the moral force of the churches should be diverted to the little issues that divide them, when it is so greatly needed for the advancement of the kingdom of God. The sin of its divisions, the folly and peril of its wasteful rivalries, lie heavy upon the mind and conscience of the Church. Now, as the smoke of ancient controversies is clearing away, Christians of every name are turning to each other with a wistful desire for a closer fellowship; and, hedged about though they are by the theologies, institutions, and ceremonials with which each communion has surrounded itself during its years of isolation, hand seeks hand across the barriers, and heart is touching heart. Among all the differences that have kept them apart, Christ's followers have never quite forgotten his prayer that they might be one, and by the memory of it they have been rebuked even while they disputed. Now the desire of Jesus is finding a new response in the hearts of his disciples, and earnestly they are seeking the means by which the ideal of their Master may be realized. Christendom is turning to its divine Leader to learn of him the things that make for the peace of the Church; and, the world around, the disciples of Jesus, with a seriousness and a degree of unanimity that herald a new day, are giving themselves to a fresh study of the mind of their Lord.

Jesus dealt in principles, not programs; in ideals, not institutions. We shall be disappointed if we approach the teachings of Jesus with the hope of finding there a specific plan for the attainment of the unity of the Church. It is impossible to quote him in support of any one of the forms in which the spirit of Christian unity is expressing itself in our day. He has nothing to say of comity or co-operation, of federation or organic unity. Jesus propounded no programs for the solution of the problems of even his own generation. But while he exhibited an indifference to the form of things, which sometimes is sorely puzzling to the practical Western mind with its faith in organization and legislation, he was profoundly concerned with the content and the spirit. When Jesus prayed for his disciples that they might be one, he was thinking, not of organic Church union, nor of any formal

unity expressed in organization, but of a vital unity
springing from the possession of a common spirit
and a common purpose. He was not thinking of
the Church, nor of sacraments, nor of ecclesiastical
polities, nor of creeds. Jesus never taught a system
of theology, nor ordained a priesthood, or even an
official ministry, nor organized a church. The purpose of Jesus was to propagate a spirit, not to estab-
lish an institution. He seems to have been willing
that the form should shape itself so long as the content and purpose were good. He spoke of "one
flock," not of "one fold,"[1] with the ecclesiastical
associations that such a term suggests—"they shall
become one flock, one shepherd." He prayed that
they who believed on him might be one, leaving it
to the spirit of love, without which no mode of
unity is possible, to determine what form would
manifest it best.

That it was a unity of *spirit* and not of organization of which Jesus was thinking is evident in the
terms in which he speaks of it. He desired such a
oneness among the disciples as he himself enjoyed
with God the Father—"that they may all be one;
even as thou, Father, art in me, and I in thee,"
The profound simplicity of his habit of thought forbids us to suppose that Jesus was speaking here in
terms of the Trinity, or of substance and essence, or

[1] John 10 : 16, R. V.

of any of the categories by which men have obscured that simplicity, and in which they have stereotyped their thinking about the divine nature. Such abstractions were foreign to him always: they belong to a later, a philosophizing age. He speaks of his unity with the Father as of a sort which disciple may have with disciple, and which must be capable of expression, therefore, in terms of human experience. "My meat is to do the will of him that sent me, and to accomplish his work;" "The words that I say unto you I speak not from myself: but the Father abiding in me doeth his works;" "My Father worketh even until now, and I work":—in such expressions lies the secret of his meaning. Evidently he was thinking of that moral and spiritual fellowship in which he was united with the Father, of a community of thought and purpose, and of partnership in service. There is no division of interest, no conflict of will, no contradiction in word, no antagonism in action between himself and the Father; and it was such unity that Jesus desired the disciples should enjoy with one another.

It was, further, a *moral* unity, cemented by the possession in common of a single moral ideal. Jesus first prayed that his disciples might be kept from the soiling influences of the world and dedicated to the truth, and then that they might dwell together in loving fellowship. Sin drives men apart and keeps them apart. It is always divisive. The greatest obstacle to Christian unity is selfishness. In proportion as the disciples of Jesus are free from worldliness and devoted to the truth will they be drawn together: the more truly Christlike they are, in other words, the more closely united they will be.

Above all, it was a *vital* unity which Jesus desired for his disciples, the bond of which should be the possession of a common spiritual experience. He yearned that the disciples should share in the divine life by which he, himself, was consciously energized, and thus be united with God and with each other. Through his presence in the lives of the disciples such a union was to be perfected; his was the life of the vine which, flowing into the branches, was to relate them to one another as parts of a single organism.

It was such unity as this, spiritual, moral, vital, that Jesus desired for his disciples in every age. He was praying not merely for the little group of the Twelve, but "for them also that believe on me through their word;" and the bond upon which Jesus depended to unite the company of his immediate disciples is the only bond that is strong enough to hold together the Church in any age. They who are not first united to Christ in loyalty and love, and to one another by the consciousness that they share a common spiritual life, will never be held together long by the artificial bonds of organization, or creed, or ecclesiastical authority. No other grounds of unity are possible in the twentieth century than those upon which was built the unity of the first.

Such a spirit manifest in the disciples Jesus believed to be essential to the fulfilment of their mission. To him it was not conceivable that the disciples could ever win the world unless they were united. A divided Church is a defeated Church. If the world is to be convinced of the divine mission and authority of the Messiah, as it so sadly needs to be convinced, his disciples must speak together, with one voice; and if the world is to be persuaded that God loves the Church of Christ and that it is entitled to represent him, then members of the Church must love one another. Truth proclaimed through faction can have no power over the world. The strongest argument for the genuineness of Christianity is lives controlled by it; and factious and contentious spirits belie the presence of Christ. The most convincing Christian apologetic is a Christian community united in love. If love for Christ is so weak in the Church that it cannot hold together those that profess it, how can it hope to win a hostile or indifferent world?

Such was the principle and ideal of unity with

which the company of disciples of Jesus started upon their world-wide career. It was natural and inevitable, in the circumstances in which they found themselves, that the little group of believers and those whom they attracted to their number, in their attempt to realize this ideal, and fulfil the prayer of their Lord, should effect some form of organization. The soul must clothe itself with a body if it is to be visible; the spirit of unity that prevailed among the disciples must disclose itself if it is to bear its message to the world.   Thus, wherever the apostles journeyed upon their preaching tours they formed their converts into local brotherhoods or churches. Paul tells us that he established churches in every city.   These churches, moreover, wherever located, were bound to one another within the fold of a more inclusive brotherhood. Throughout the apostolic age, while there were churches at Antioch, at Corinth, at Laodicea, and elsewhere, they were united in more than a mere confederation.   From the beginning all Christians thought of themselves, not simply as members of a local congregation at Philippi or Ephesus, but as members of the universal Christian Church of which the church in a particular city was only a local manifestation.   The earliest Christians thought of their community as a family, and conversion marked their adoption into the household of faith.   Wherever the Church spread, this conception of its character continued, and Christians everywhere were brethren, and members of the same family in Christ.[1]

The desire of the Apostle Paul to promote this sentiment is evident throughout all his epistles. In founding churches among the Gentiles he was not, as he conceived it, establishing independent organizations, but was adding to the Christian family. The Gentiles were to be grafted in among the Jewish Christians and to become "partaker with them of the root of the fatness of the olive tree."[2] It was Paul's desire, not merely to promote the unity of the Church, but to secure the co-operation of all the churches that he founded with the Jerusalem church in particular, and it was because that union was endangered that he was caused such anxiety at the time of the Council at Jerusalem. It is true that the unity of spirit between the Gentile churches and the church at Jerusalem was never ideal; but the earnest desire of the apostle that it should be cemented is evident in his emphasis upon the great collection for the poor saints at Jerusalem, which he urged so strongly upon the churches that he had founded, in the hope that this evidence of good-will might bind the parent church to them in closer fellowship.

[1] Cf. McGiffert, *The Apostolic Age*, p. 636 ff.
[2] Rom. 11 : 17 ff.

It is of the Church universal that Paul is thinking when he speaks of it as "the body of Christ,"[1] and uses the figure as an argument particularly against the sin of schism. "For as the body is one, and hath many members, and all the members of the body, being many, are one body; so also," he declares, "is Christ. For in one Spirit were we all baptized into one body, whether Jews or Greeks, whether bond or free; and were all made to drink of one Spirit." While he finds abundant scope for variety and diversity within the unity of the Church, as there are differences of function and honor among the members of the body, he urges the utmost consideration and mutual forbearance among the constituent members in order "that there should be no schism in the body." He strongly deprecates the forming of sects under the leadership and name of human teachers as doing violence to the unity of the body of Christ, for that Christ should be divided is to him both an abhorrent and an impossible idea.[2] He continually urges his converts that they endeavor to "keep the unity of the Spirit in the bond of peace." "There is one body," he declares, "and one Spirit, even as also ye were called in one hope of your calling; one Lord, one faith, one baptism, one God and Father of all, who is over all, and through all, and in all." The various gifts dis-

[1] I. Cor. 12 : 12–27.   [2] I. Cor. 1 : 13 ff.

tributed by the ascended Christ to believers have for the goal of their exercise "the perfecting of the saints unto the work of ministering, unto the building up of the body of Christ: till we all attain unto the unity of the faith, and of the knowledge of the Son of God, unto a full-grown man, unto the measure of the stature of the fulness of Christ."[1]

During the apostolic period the unity of the Church, it is evident, was one of spirit and not of organization. Differences of church polity appear even within New Testament times. The organization of the earliest churches was the simplest possible, and was often affected by local condition and custom. The scattered Christian communities were held together, not by any scheme of organization or governmental authority exercised from without, nor by subscription to a single creedal statement; but by possession, in common, of the ideal of a united Church. As members of the one body of Christ they were bound to love their brethren. There was no central government, no ecclesiastical hierarchy, no compulsion but the compulsion of love. That the separate churches did not diverge and become altogether independent of one another in their developing life was due to the possession of a single ideal and spirit. Their sense of unity was fostered by the visits of apostles and prophets from

[1] Eph. 4 : 3-6; 12, 13.

the parent church, by an interchange of visits on the part of local leaders, by the circulation of Christian literature among the churches, particularly the letters of the apostles, and most of all by the persecution which they endured together at the hands of Jew and Gentile. While these cemented the union, they did not create it. It was a purely ideal unity, dependent upon the belief of Christians everywhere that their Lord meant them to be one, and that love for Him involved it. Says Prof. Glover, in his *Conflict of Religions in the Early Roman Empire*, "Two things stand out, when we study the character of early Christianity—its great complexity and variety, and its unity in the personality of Jesus of Nazareth."

Several generations passed before the process began that was to transform this spiritual unity of the first disciples into a "catholicity," which depended for its expression upon a form of church polity. Gradually the independence of the local church was surrendered to a diocesan bishop as the visible representative of the universal Church; however, with this outward appearance of unity there was no corresponding growth in the spirit of it. The *spirit* of unity that sprang from a wealth of love and the sense of a common mission and allegiance slowly lost ground before the advance of a *visible* and *formal* unity manifested in a hierarchy

4

of church officials and in authoritative creeds and councils. Toward the close of the apostolic age unity was more and more secured by the simple method of excluding all who differed with the ruling majority, until the Church was united, indeed, but had ceased to be comprehensive.

Most of the dissenting groups of the first three centuries were actuated by a desire to return to the simplicity of the faith and order of the apostles, but their failure to secure the favor of the dominant majority branded them as heretics, and pronounced their doom. "Many schisms arose in the early ages," wrote Dr. Philip Schaff, "before and after the Council of Nicea. Almost every great controversy resulted in the excommunication of the defeated party, who organized a separate sect, if they were not exterminated by the civil power. The Nestorians, Armenians, Jacobites, and Copts, who seceded from the Greek Orthodox Church, continue to this day as relics of dead controversies."[1] The beginning of the age of Catholicism marked the beginning of sectarianism through the perpetual protest of successive groups of Christians who resisted the drift of the leaders of the Church away from the doctrines and practices of the apostolic age.

It is no part of our purpose to review the history

[1] Schaff, *The Reunion of Christendom*, p. 5.

of succeeding ages, or to indicate in more than outline the steps by which a formal unity was secured
through the development of a compact and powerful
ecclesiastical organization, and the promulgation of
authoritative dogmas. The Church was compelled
to pay the price of a growing popularity in the gradual materialization of its ideals. Among the thousands who flocked into its fold were many who were
imperfectly weaned from paganism, and who
brought with them their pagan ideals and ceremonies. The pressure of the intellectualism of the
Greco-Roman world, in the midst of which it lived,
tempted the Church to formulate its creeds in the
language of the current philosophies. The struggle
of the Church with its most formidable antagonist,
Gnosticism, and its attendant errors, appeared to
the Church to compel it to define with the utmost
exactness the essentials of orthodoxy, and to emphasize its distinctive ceremonies as necessary to
salvation. The free and plastic polity of the New
Testament was early abandoned and the Church
was modeled upon the Empire. The bishop ceased
to be the overseer of a single parish and became the
governor of a district, like the Roman proconsul.
The college of cardinals corresponded to the senate,
and the pope was established on Cæsar's seat to
rule a spiritual and temporal empire. The spirit
of the gospel was imprisoned within semi-legal

forms; penance took the place of penitence; orthodoxy became submission to the councils, and heresy
was identified with disobedience to them. Faith
lost its experimental, vital character, and became
intellectual assent to dogma; while the simple
ordinances observed by the early Church developed
into sacraments endowed with a magical efficacy.
Freedom and spontaneity in worship gave way
before the exclusive use of liturgies. Where moral
suasion failed to secure unity, force was substituted;
and individual liberty was sacrificed upon the altar
of authority.

At length, after the long sleep of the Dark Ages,
the light of the Renaissance broke through the night,
not only awakening the minds of men to a new appreciation of their heritage in art and literature, which
had been so long neglected, but rousing the slumber-
ing consciences of men to claim again that spiritual
liberty which was the birthright of the early Church.
The new learning stimulated the spirit of criticism;
a new nationalism stirred the spirit of revolt; the
gospel, rediscovered, kindled again the embers of
the apostolic faith in the hearts of thousands; and
the spirit of man entered upon a new career of freedom. The Reformation shattered in pieces the
formal unity of the Church. The right of every
man to interpret the Scriptures for himself was
asserted in the face of arrogant authority, and men

claimed again the privilege of access to the divine Father without the intervention of priest, or saint, or institution.

This marked the beginning of the modern age. The ferment of the new wine broke the ancient wine-skins, and new bottles were needed to receive it. For four centuries a large part of Christendom has enjoyed a measure of religious freedom, and the spirit of man has created a multitude of institutions through which the religious impulse has found expression. Beyond computation has been the gain of the race from the rediscovery of those formative ideas which were the dynamic of the Reformation. Yet even freedom has its dangers, and may easily degenerate into license. Individuality unrestrained tends toward self-assertion and eccentricity. The revolt against an unnatural and compulsory uniformity has not been attended by the recovery of the secret of that spiritual unity which held together the apostolic Church, for the preservation of which the Master prayed.

In America, which has long enjoyed the blessings of that religious liberty of which Roger Williams was the first exponent, the tendency toward division and subdivision has gone the farthest, until, in its 143 denominations of Christians, it would seem that every possible difference of doctrine and procedure must be represented. The "dissidence of dissent" has reached a *reductio ad absurdum*. In the dissipation of resources, the duplication of agencies, the competition in over-churched communities and the neglect of needy areas which such division of its forces entails, Protestantism has passed the danger point, and its power to achieve the thing for which it was created has already suffered loss. Energy that ought to have been directed toward the redemption of the world has been spent in wasteful rivalry, and even in recrimination. The seamless robe of Christ is rent, and the Church, his body, is torn into fragments. A babel of discordant voices threatens to drown the voice of prophecy; every vagary claims the right of utterance; and under cloak of the right of private judgment the duties of tolerance and charity are in danger of being forgotten. This is the weakness and the scandal of Protestantism.

As the magnitude of the missionary task at home and abroad is more fully grasped, there has come a despair of success except through the united efforts of a united Church. They who pray, "Thy kingdom come," are forced also to pray for the servants of the kingdom "that they may all be one." The world will never be won to Christ by guerrilla warfare, by disorganized bands of partisans; but only by an ordered campaign of disciplined troops that advance together. The native Christians upon the foreign field, the first fruits of the missionary enterprise, and missionaries upon the frontier in the home land, are the foremost advocates of a policy of union and co-operation, of the lack of which they have been the most unfortunate victims.

The problems of social life that so largely occupy the thought of Christendom to-day are a challenge to the Church to unite for their solution. The ills from which society is suffering are more than economic, and economic readjustments alone will not suffice to correct them. Believing, as it does, that it holds the secret of a real brotherhood of man whose attainment is fundamental to the solution of every social problem, the Church owes a duty to society; but it never can perform that duty until it shall itself incarnate the spirit of brotherhood and speak with the power and weight of a united testimony.

Slowly the conviction is being borne in upon the consciousness of Christendom that there is no future for a divided Church. "An unbelieving world," Dr. John R. Mott has said, "is the price we are paying for a divided Christianity." The forces of evil on every side are consolidating in an unholy alliance. The children of darkness are wiser far in their generation than the children of light. The Church is urged to a crusade the desperate character of which daily becomes more clear; and, if Tancred and Baldwin are to war with one another and spend the strength of the crusading army, the hosts of the Saracens may well expect an easy victory. A thousand voices within and without are calling upon the Church to unite, and to combine its forces. The measure in which the people of God of the twentieth century respond to that appeal is the supreme test of modern Christianity.

So in the midst of the confusion and noise there may be heard a still, small voice speaking with an insistence that compels attention, that is deeply moving the heart of Christendom to-day. It is the voice of the Lord of the Church praying still, as he once prayed in the upper room for his disciples, "that they may all be one; even as thou, Father, art in me, and I in thee, that they also may be in us: that the world may believe that thou didst send me." Men are turning hopefully to a study of the sources of the unity of the early Church, that dwelt in a holy fellowship cemented by loyalty and love, and are daring to believe that what has been may be again. If Jesus prayed for the unity of his disciples it must be a practicable ideal; and, if so, it shall be achieved! Somehow, it knows not yet how, the prayer of its Lord must be fulfilled by the Church. What Jesus prayed for, his disciples must work for. Without forfeiting again the benefits of a freedom so dearly bought, the disciples of Jesus must be one.

Great opportunities await the advent of the new

catholicity. A world weary of the burdens of increasing armaments, and torn with the horrors of unrighteous war sighs for universal peace. An awakening democracy, rising to seize the reins of power in every land, must be spiritualized if it is to fulfil its lofty destiny. The victims of materialism and greed, ground beneath the iron heel of a social and economic system built in the interest of a favored few, call aloud to the Church for succor. Everywhere the heathen world holds out manacled hands of entreaty, beseeching to be freed from the iron bands of superstition. And in the face of the need of a crucified humanity, a disunited Church is helpless. It is the imperative duty of the disciples of Jesus to get together! Reluctance is disloyalty to the Lord who prayed for them, and treachery to the world for which he died!

THE PASSING OF THE SECTARIAN
SPIRIT

Unity not to be secured at the sacrifice of principle.—Characteristic differences considered unimportant by various denominations.—Rise of denominations in age of individualism.—The new social organism—its influence upon the Church.—Examples of petty differences and harsh invectives.—Changing world conditions forecast spiritual changes.—Co-operation in theological education.—Church must meet its problems.—Conditions in America most conducive to co-operation.

CHAPTER III

THE Christian world is no longer willing to believe that spiritual liberty must be maintained at the price of the waste and loss which are the result of its divisions. Is it not possible, men are asking everywhere, for Protestantism to conserve the principles that are precious to it, and that constitute its strength, and yet find a way to unite its scattered forces and heal its schisms? May it not even continue to cherish the best for which denominationalism has stood, and still be freed from the bonds of a narrowly sectarian and partisan spirit?

It may be readily granted that catholicity might be bought at too great a cost. There is no magic in mere unity that would compensate for the surrender of that liberty of conscience, and that insistence upon the spiritual competency of the individual which have been the glory of the Protestant movement. It needs no argument to prove that spiritual vigor and fidelity to conviction are of more value than anything that could be received in exchange for them. The danger, however, that Protestants will take a backward step and betray the cause for

61

which their fathers bled and died for the sake of any form of unity is exceedingly remote. If a new unity of the Church could be secured to-morrow by the surrender of principle or such a sacrifice of spiritual liberty as was demanded by the so-called Catholic ages of the past, it would be broken the day after to-morrow by a new Reformation, for the free spirit of man would assert itself again and the artificial bonds would break like tow at the touch of fire.

It is charged that much of the current advocacy of the cause of Christian unity is merely the expression of a lack of any definite religious conviction whatsoever. Without a doubt, to one who thinks it does not matter what one believes, all shades of belief look very much alike. The Romans of the Empire were broadly tolerant in religious matters, and exceedingly hospitable to new religions, so that the addition of another god or two to the pantheon provoked little comment; but it was because in Rome faith in the gods was almost dead. It is possible, indeed, to be so broad as to be shallow, and tolerance may be only another name for indifference. "We put blinders upon horses," says Dr. Parkhurst, "just so that they may not take broad views of things, but may go forward." Such considerations as these, however, may easily be made an excuse for moral cowardice and spiritual bigotry.

A most cordial recognition of the right of other men to their convictions is surely compatible with the most loyal allegiance to one's own. It would be humiliating to be compelled to confess that men must be purblind or cease to advance. "A faith dependent upon blinkers and fetters," Sir Oliver Lodge has said, "is not likely, in a progressive age, to last many generations. Anchorage to a submerged rock is not safe amid rising waters."

Any process of spiritual enlargement is attended with peril. The moment of greatest danger for the "chambered nautilus," of which Holmes has sung, was doubtless that at which, its outgrown shell discarded and its new and larger dwelling not yet constructed, it lay exposed to every passing foe. At such a point the cause of Christian unity stands to-day. Nevertheless, whatever danger there may be that the larger sympathy, which longs for co-operation and unity with Christians of every name, may lapse into an invertebrate and molluscoid sort of good feeling that lacks force sufficient to accomplish anything, or even to protect itself from destruction, there is still greater danger that a narrowly denominational loyalty may degenerate into mere pride, obstinacy, and prejudice. There is many a man who sincerely loves the denomination to which he belongs,—because he was reared within it, or found Christ through its ministry, or has labored within its ranks until its interests have become identified with his own, or because he believes that of all denominations it is most faithful to New Testament teaching,—but who finds it impossible to ignore the fact that a multitude of other men, as sincere and as Christian as he, make identical claims for their own denominations and profess as great a loyalty to them.   Each one among the larger Protestant denominations stoutly claims to stand upon the New Testament platform, and justly prides itself upon a record of useful service. And here is a curious circumstance that must impress itself upon the mind of every thoughtful man, that while the distinctive principles of each denomination seem to its adherents to be so important and so significant for all the world, and not to be sacrificed, they appear, in the degree in which they are distinctive, to be of very little consequence to other denominations, whose members nevertheless exhibit all the essential marks of Christian character and usefulness. Meanwhile the cause of the kingdom suffers irreparable loss from the division of its forces. Reflection upon such considerations as these is breaking down the barriers of prejudice that once separated denominationalists from each other.

While, therefore, the current advocacy of Christian unity may be due occasionally to spiritual impoverishment or to latitudinarianism, indifference toward the issue, or the failure boldly to advocate it, is more often due to timidity, or to ignorance, or to inertia and a blind conservatism, or to fear of the denominational sheriffs and the editors and officials who are constantly occupied in keeping the denominational fences in repair.

There is a zeal that believes the peculiarity of a denomination to be the best thing about it, and that confuses religion with the ability to pronounce denominational shibboleths, and that rejoices in principles in proportion as they are distinctive, just as there is a patriotism that cries, "My country, right or wrong!" To those who accept this position, the virtue of religion lies in "the dissidence of dissent." Growing up, however, by the side of what President Butler has called "the international mind" is an interdenominational consciousness which must be reckoned with to-day, which, while loyal to distinctive tenets, sees over and beyond them, and recognizes the more imperative claims of a higher loyalty to the interests of the kingdom of God.

Denominational divisions took their rise during the period marked by the discovery of the individual. It is among the glories of the Reformation that it asserted the freedom and competency of man as man in the domain of religion, and thus promulgated a principle which, spreading into other fields,

5

has wrought mightily for his emancipation from
every form of thraldom. It was a splendid and
epoch-making discovery, that of the rights and dignity of man, and it has transformed not only the
religious world, but the worlds of industry and of
politics, shaping legislation and government and
social custom and economic institutions and making
always for liberty. But we are passing to-day out
of the era of individualism into that of collectivism.
We would not part with an atom of what we have
gained, nor ever again lose sight of the individual,
nor permit the exploitation of his rights; but we
are now making a new discovery,—that of the community. Over against the rights of a fraction of
society is the right of society as a whole. The free
competition of individuals must be restrained and
regulated in the interest of the welfare of the community. This is the new emphasis which is exercis-
ing the profoundest influence in every realm of
thought and conduct. But, while the spirit of individualism was a product of the religious instinct
and first expressed itself in the religious realm, the
collective ideal arose in the social and economic realm
and is only slowly making its way in the sphere of
religion. Some day the idea of "private religion,"
with the unrestrained rights of competition which
it involves, will go the way of that conception of
"private business" which, with all the arrogant

disregard of community interests that it represents, is retreating before the advance of the spirit of democracy.

This change of emphasis from the individual to the social organism which characterizes our times has relegated to comparative insignificance many of the issues that once divided the ranks of Christendom. Interest has shifted from creeds to conduct, and from a purely personal salvation to one that shall save the individual indeed, but that aims also at the saving of society. Men are weary of treating symptoms only, and in every avenue of activity are seeking to discover causes and to deal with them directly. The methods of social science are preventive rather than merely curative, and men now endeavor to purify the stream at its source rather than to filter it at the outlet. Instead of merely relieving poverty, they seek to discover and to remove the causes of poverty. The old method in medicine was to wait until the patient had contracted a disease and then to exhaust the resources of science in the effort to cure him. The modern method is to attack disease at its source through sanitation and hygiene. This is increasingly becoming the method of religion. The Church is more interested than it once was in the conditions that tempt to sin, and is giving attention to the means of prevention as well as to those of cure. As has often been said, it is well to play the Good Samaritan and to bind up the wounds of the traveler beset by thieves, but it is necessary also to illumine the highway from Jericho to Jerusalem, and thoroughly to police it, so that the traveler may pursue his journey in safety.

From this shifting of emphasis, then, there has come a new appraisal of many of the points of difference that have divided the forces of Christendom. Few of the distinctive denominational tenets concern matters over which men with red blood in their veins can become enthusiastic to-day. Seldom do they coincide with a burning conviction of living men. They lie on the periphery and not at the center of religious interest; or they are relics of outgrown controversies. The Church, driven forward by the impact of the new spirit of the times, has left most of them behind. How remote at the present time seem some of the differences that once divided Christian people—minute points of doctrine, it may be, or of ritual observance! In one of the smaller cities of the Atlantic coast stand two Presbyterian churches, facing each other, upon opposite sides of the street. They are the result of a division that occurred in one of them almost two generations ago because a portion of the congregation held to a "mediate atonement" and the other to an "immediate atonement," distinctions which few Christians to-day would understand without recourse to a theological dictionary. At the beginning of the eighteenth century the Baptists of Delaware withdrew from fellowship with the Baptists of Philadelphia because the latter did not "hold to the laying on of hands." Doubtless many of the present differences will some day seem as remote. Questions of the validity of orders, of postures and rubrics, of stoles and altar cloths, and of ecclesiastical millinery in general, of forms of polity and of modes of ordinances, once the center of bitter controversy, are of little consequence to-day. Men are weary, also, of spending precious time in "manicuring one another's theology," as Dr. Shailer Mathews has phrased it. The questions in which the present generation is interested are such as housing, temperance, the purification of politics, the extension of democracy, the protection of youth, the abolition of poverty, the suppression of commercialized vice, and the building up of a real Kingdom of God upon earth through the transformation of men into the likeness of Christ, no one of which undertakings is distinctive of any single denomination. These are the great enthusiasms; and they are not divisive, but are common to men of every Christian faith.

Sectarianism in its extreme form is dying to-day for lack of nourishment, as a limb would die if a tourniquet were drawn tightly about it, shutting off the blood supply. Where are the doughty champions who once were ready at a moment's notice to descend into the arena and break a lance in the cause of some denominational peculiarity? They are gone,—gone with the ancient bitterness which tainted the atmosphere which they breathed. The leading evangelical preachers of the latter part of the eighteenth century and the first half of the nineteenth were "fighting parsons," with a freedom in their choice of verbal weapons that appals us to-day.

"Sidney, in his biography of Rowland Hill, quotes these among the epithets applied to the 'Calvinists' by 'these two meek and loving gentlemen, Messrs. John and Charles Wesley': 'devil's factors, Satan's synagogues, children of the old, roaring, hellish murderer who believe his lie, advocates for sin, witnesses for the father of lies, blasphemers, Satan-sent preachers.'" "Among the pet names applied by Hill to Wesley were, 'the lying apostle of the Foundry,' 'a designing wolf,' and 'a dealer in stolen wares.' And to cap the climax, the sentence of Hill's may be quoted in which Wesley is called 'as unprincipled as a rook, and as silly as a jackdaw, first pilfering his neighbor's plumage, and then going proudly forth displaying his borrowed tail to the eyes of a laughing world.'"[1] Some of these old-time saints had what approached a real genius for billingsgate, but we do not reckon it to-day among their virtues.

Arrogant and extravagant claims on the part of large or small sects that think themselves to be the particular favorites of heaven and to have got a corner on salvation are discounted to-day as soon as uttered. The world has as little patience with them as had Ruskin with the preacher of the type that he ran across in a little chapel in Turin. "A little squeaking idiot," he says, "was preaching to an audience of old women and three louts that they were the only children of God in Turin; and that the people of Turin, outside the chapel, and that all the people in the world, out of sight of Monte Viso, would be damned!" Self-laudation is a mark of decadence wherever met. Men are very definitely convinced that they are not to be saved by right thinking merely, and that religion is not identical with theology: creeds, therefore, do not hold the pre-eminent place that once was accorded them. A form of church polity, also, like a horse, "is a vain thing for safety." It is growing harder every year to maintain the denominational fences. Deplore it though we may, members of one communion, upon changing their residence, pass with in-

[1] "The Battle of the Saints," G. F. Greene, *Outlook*, April 26, 1902, p. 1012. Quoted in *What Must the Church Do to be Saved?* by F. Marion Simms.

creasing ease into membership in another, and are not held as strongly as at one time by the distinctive features of the sect to which they gave their first allegiance. They join with a growing frequency the nearest church, or that which they think is fulfilling with most efficiency what they believe to be the real mission of religion. And while the most apparent differences between the churches are losing something of their significance, other marks of divergence are appearing. Every communion has its liberal and conservative wings, and, as the perpendicular lines between denominations grow more faint, the horizontal lines of cleavage which cut through them all appear more clearly. There is often more real sympathy and spiritual fellowship between liberals or conservatives of different denominations than exists between liberals and conservatives within a single body. This is a phenomenon of much significance, the ultimate consequence of which it is too early to prophesy.

Such indications suggest that there is to come, perhaps within our time, a startling realignment of Christian forces. The world of thought and of action moves with a bewildering rapidity. Ideas rise, gain acceptance, spread, and are now put into execution within a period incommensurably more brief than the process would have taken half or even a quarter of a century ago. We catch our breath at the speed at which the world of thought is moving. Witness the changes in political ideals and practices in recent years both in our own country and throughout the world. Democracy in England advances with giant strides. Oriental Japan is transformed within a decade, and has become a world power. "Better fifty years of Europe than a cycle of Cathay," we used to quote; but China has overtaken Europe and has turned face about almost in a night. In America the political and social radicalism of yesterday is the conservatism of to-day. The impossible is becoming the actual, and the dream of the political prophet having been achieved becomes the basis of more radical proposals still. The world is rapidly coming to the conclusion that what is right is possible, and the laggard faith of the Church is being shamed into action. If a larger measure of Christian unity is right, if it is the ideal of the Lord of the Church, then it must come, and none can say it nay.

We may profitably sit at the feet of the Christian Chinese in such a matter. Free from the prejudices that have been inherited from the past by the Christians of the West, it may well be that they are able to judge more impartially than we as to the character of the causes that divide us. If these men, many of whom have proved their sincerity and fidelity to the Christian faith by tests more severe than any to which we have been subjected; if they, who are as able intellectually as ourselves, and who have been willing to lay down their lives for the faith, have deliberately concluded that the differences that divide our Western Christianity into fragments are non-essential, it may be worth while for us to reconsider them. And if we can contemplate without alarm the disappearance of our points of difference in the churches we have founded in Eastern lands, is it too much to conclude that they need not, in their present form, be perpetuated forever in the West?

Surely there is possible a fellowship and cooperation of the closest nature which does not require the slightest unfaithfulness to individual convictions. Already in some of our theological seminaries students of many denominations gather. They study homiletics, theology, church history, ethics, and sociology together: in such subjects there is general agreement. Upon the subjects wherein there is disagreement, special teachers are appointed who present the points of view of particular denominations. It happens, as was to be expected, that the students come forth to take up the work of the denominations to which they belong,— Presbyterians, Congregationalists, Baptists, Methodists, or Episcopalians,—as they entered, but wiser and broader, with a richer experience and a wider sympathy and fellowship, through contact with those of other faiths. A large measure of co-operation in theological education is already possible. Will the witness of the denominations to the peculiar truths which they conceive themselves severally to hold in trust be weakened if they mingle together in fellowship, worship, and service? Is it not at least conceivable that a Baptist's testimony to the symbolism and spiritual value of the apostolic mode of baptism, or a Presbyterian's witness to the necessity of a sound theology, or an Episcopalian's emphasis upon institutional religion would be quite as potent for good if they freely united in a single church, for worship and service, as it can possibly be while each remains a member of a church composed of those only who already have identical thoughts and is fenced off from contact with those who differ? Differences of conviction, quite as serious as any that divide denominations from one another, are frequently found within the membership of a single denomination without any impairment of fellowship. Why may not members of several denominations, therefore, unite without discord in a community church, each retaining liberty to speak the truth in love as he sees it, and to adhere to his distinctive theology? One of the causes of our divisions lies in the fact that they arose in an age when our modern methods of intercommunication were unknown, and men with different conceptions of truth could not easily meet; and truth is not learned in isolation. The yeast must be mixed with the lump if it is to leaven it. One of the penalties of our separation is that we fail to understand each other, and to appreciate the truths that we severally hold. A community church in which various denominations combine ought to develop a new and more comprehensive theology and polity and practice, as it absorbs the best that each of its constituent elements has to contribute.

Whatever the method, some way must be found by which Christianity can meet its problems with united front. The present stress of the Church has made it hospitable to the thought of the unification of its forces. "To be enthusiastic about the Church in its present condition," writes Prof. A. B. Bruce, "is impossible." "There is such a thing as a religious crisis in America," says a careful observer, "however much we may scoff at the idea." In view of the serious problems which the Church is facing— the arrogance of vice, the federation of all forms of evil, the growth of unbelief and indifference, waning congregations, the alienation of the workingman— how pitifully small and sad seem its fine discriminations of doctrine, its ecclesiastical frills and furbelows, its liturgical refinements and delicacies of deportment in worship, its petty scruples as to washing of cups and pots and tables, its Pharisaic pretensions and hairsplittings, its competitive ambitions, its insistence upon forms and ceremonies, and its disputes as to the possession of the requisite authority to do the things that so greatly need to be done, which are the cause or the effect of its unfortunate divisions! Like the American colonies in the days of the Revolution, the churches of America must hang together or they will hang separately. It is imperative that they should make up their differences and join ranks. As the British ships drew near the French at the battle of Trafalgar, Admiral Nelson called to his flagship captains, Collingwood and Hardy, who up to that time had been bitter enemies, and commanded them to shake hands, saying, as he pointed to the French ships of the line, "Gentlemen, there is your enemy!"

If an effective co-operative union of Christian forces is possible anywhere in the world, surely it should be possible in America. In a free and democratic country, where, in theory at least, every man counts for one and no man for more than one, whose political institutions are founded upon the town meeting, where men of every faith and of different ideas meet to further the interests of the community, setting aside their personal preferences and submitting to the will of the majority, the ability to think and act in common is instilled into the very blood. Here is no established Church to foster bitterness or create jealousies.   Freedom of religious conviction is guaranteed to every citizen.   Here are the opportunities of a country a large part of which is still new, and the pressing needs of great frontier districts still unsupplied with religious privileges.

There is possible a co-operative union which sacrifices nothing that is essential, and slowly we are finding our way toward it.   He who furthers this end, however slight may be his contribution, is engaged in the noblest work to which he can set his hand.   "To effect one real step in the direction of reunion," said Mr. Gladstone, "after the results of the last five hundred years, would be enough to lead any man to lay down his head and die contentedly."

THE GROWTH OF THE SPIRIT OF
CHRISTIAN UNITY

Place of love in Christian unity.—Study of church history conduces to unity: it reveals both imperfections and triumphs in each denomination.—Teaching of the New Testament and example of the apostolic Church.—Group individuality.—Unity of Christian scholarship.—Doctrinal unity.—Ethical unity.—Unity in charitable activities.—Unity in the aim and purpose of the Church.—Christian love the secret of unity.

CHAPTER IV

SPECIFIC plans and programs for the unification of the forces of Christendom are advanced on every hand; but before any one of these can be put into operation, however practical it may be or theoretically wise, there must be a more thorough cultivation of the spirit of Christian love. The unity for which we pray, when it comes, will not be a manufacture, but a growth. Like the Kingdom of God it "cometh not with observation: neither shall they say, Lo, here! or lo, there!" for, behold, the substance of Christian unity "is within you." World Conferences on Faith and Order, Chicago-Lambeth Proposals, Denominational Commissions on Comity or Christian Union are, without doubt, helpful; but these never can accomplish anything unless they find within the churches a deepening spirit of Christian love to which they can make their appeal. The consummation of any scheme of union, whether of local churches or of denominations, would be, like a marriage without affection, a calamity and foredoomed to failure, if it were not the fruit of Christian love. And love cannot be forced or hurried: it

6   81

must lead, not follow. The spirit of co-operation is not always most prevalent where circumstances seem most to favor it. It is less evident, sometimes, in communities of few churches that do not need to compete than in others of many churches in which competition can hardly be avoided. No apparent necessity can compel churches or denominations into co-operation where the spirit of love is lacking. Never were truer words spoken than those of John Owen, one of the greatest of Puritan divines, when he said, "I should be very sorry that any man living should outgo me in desires that all who fear God throughout the world, especially in these nations, were of one way as well as of one heart. I know that I desire it sincerely. But I verily believe that when God shall accomplish it, it will be the *effect* of love and not the *cause* of love. There is not a greater vanity in the world than to drive men into a particular profession and then suppose that love will be the necessary outcome of it; to think that if, by sharp rebukes, by cutting, bitter expressions, they can drive men into such and such practices, love will certainly ensue."

It would be worse than useless for the denominations to come together in organic unity until they have so far reached a common understanding that it would be possible for them to live and labor harmoniously together. The situation that would result, if so premature a union were effected, would be as awkward as that described by the Russian fabulist, Ivan Kriloff, in his story of *The Swan, the Crayfish, and the Pike:*

"A crayfish, pike, and swan agreed one day
To pull a cartload all together;
So, harnessed each to his own tether,
They pull with might and main!
Alas! 'Tis all in vain!
The load seemed light enough; but in the sky
The swan soared high;
The crayfish always backward ran,
And, in the pond, the pike to pull began.
Which was to blame? Which right? We cannot say;
But still the cartload stays there, to this day!"

The largest contribution that any man can make, therefore, to the cause of Christian unity at this stage in its progress is the promotion of mutual acquaintance, understanding, and appreciation among the divided communions of Christendom. The ignorance of intelligent men as to the spirit and tenets of other denominations than their own is as curious as it is sad. There is no ardent denominationalist who has not, at times, been chagrined at the misrepresentation that his denomination has suffered at the hand of some sincere but ignorant representative of another denomination; and such misrepresentation tends, as much as any other single cause, to perpetuate the spirit of division. Every seminary curriculum ought to contain, together with a course upon comparative religions, a course upon comparative denominationalism. Instinctively we shrink from what is strange and unfamiliar, and friendship is impossible without acquaintance. We should find ourselves much more closely in agreement with those of other Christian bodies if only we fully understood them. The Talmud says: "Walking on the mountains one day I saw a form which I took to be a beast; coming nearer I saw it was a man; approaching nearer still I found it was my brother!" We never can understand our neighbor until we get his point of view. Standing by his side and looking at truth from his angle, it is marvelous how reasonable his views appear. Again and again, in the reports of the Continuation Committee Conferences, lately held in the Orient, stress is laid upon the importance of mutual acquaintance and the mutual esteem and understanding that flow from it; as at the China National Convention at Shanghai, where one of the resolutions called for "the fresh study by all Christians of the faith and order held by those who differ from them, in order to promote cordial mutual understanding; and the holding of local conferences from time to time for the discussion of the important subject of Christian unity."[1]

[1] *The Continuation Conferences in Asia*, p. 329.

Many influences to-day are drawing the churches together. Among these must be counted the fuller light that is being thrown upon the history and origin of the Christian bodies. An impartial study of Christian history is a great destroyer of both pride and prejudice. It will destroy pride, because no perfect church is discovered anywhere in the record. The earliest church-members were charged with grievous sins in the writings of their leaders. There are few churches which have not been persecutors in their turn, and those not employing the carnal weapons of fire and sword have been guilty of misrepresentation and bitter controversy. On the other hand it will destroy prejudice, because the story of every church is fragrant with the spirit of self-sacrifice and adorned by noble lives that have been lived within its fellowship. All modern lines of spiritual descent are seen to converge in the first century; all the divided branches of the Church inherit the tradition of the unbroken unity of the first disciples of the Lord. All modern communions claim as their own the great leaders of the early centuries. Christ's presence has been manifest in every church and in every age. The study of history, therefore, wonderfully softens asperity. Viewed from a distance remote from the occasions of division and strife, the causes of controversy lose their sharp angles: distinctions, once seen in bold relief, melt into one another in the mellow light of time. Many a divisive theory has been proved to be untenable as the results of historical study have become more accurate.

Modern scholarship, as applied also to the study of the Bible, makes strongly for Christian unity. It reveals in a stronger light the unity that prevailed in the primitive Church, and upon how broad a basis it rested. The unity of the first disciples was evidently founded, not upon identity of theological belief, for there was more than one school of thought in the Church of the apostles, nor upon uniformity in church polity, since every form of organization may find its prototype in apostolic times, nor upon similarity in forms of worship, for, side by side with the freest expression of religious emotion, fragments of liturgy and creed are found embedded in the inspired writings, but upon loyalty to the one Lord of the Church, and on fidelity to the cause of his kingdom on earth. It was "unity of the Spirit in the bond of peace," unity amid diversity, and compatible with the fullest liberty of development. It consisted in no hard-and-fast mechanical uniformity of method imposed by heaven according to a prearranged plan, but was the outgrowth of experience and the instrument of efficiency. As the method of the early Church was plastic and adapted to the particular conditions with which it dealt, so there is nothing in God's Word that forbids further adaptations of method to new conditions as they appear. Its emphasis is upon unity, and not upon the means by which unity shall be secured; and he who sacrifices the end to a mistaken loyalty to a method is false to the spirit of the Bible. We are beginning to see that the great laws of social evolution that shaped the institutions of Old Testament times apply also to the period of the formation of the Church and to its history through the ages, and that many of the incidents of that history and of the particular forms that characterized it are accidental and not essential.

The older view of the Bible, with its doctrine of a mechanical and verbal inspiration and a completed revelation, has tended to perpetuate the divisions of Christendom: the modern view that the Scriptures contain the record of a progressive revelation, communicated through the experiences of men dominated by the influence of the Spirit of God, promises to be among the most potent of future influences making for the unity of the Church. The temptation of those who held the earlier view was to attempt to harmonize the various conceptions of truth presented in the New Testament, to abstract from each its points of distinction and individuality, and to "conventionalize" them into a single pattern or summary of doctrine to serve as a standard of

orthodoxy for all time. There could be little room
for differences of conviction as to either doctrine or
polity within a Church dominated by such a method.
Naturally those who could not subscribe to the
standards were forced out of the Church. The
modern view, which recognizes a development of
doctrine within the New Testament, and differences
of conception among the leaders of the early Church,
finds larger room for variations of belief within the
Church to-day, and for a continued development
within it, in both doctrine and polity, under the guidance of the Spirit of God. God has not made here
and there, only, a revelation of himself to man.
Such revelations are not confined to particular ages,
nor to a single collection of books, nor are they re-
stricted to a single method. God is continually
revealing himself and his purposes, and in every succeeding age more fully and clearly, as men are better
able to receive them. "God, having of old time
spoken unto the fathers in the prophets by divers
portions and in divers manners," hath in these days
spoken unto us, who, like the apostles and the
prophets of old, may enjoy the influences of his
indwelling Spirit. To the Christian consciousness
may come to-day new truths that shall develop new
forms through which they shall express themselves.
We have a right to trust the guidance of that Spirit
of God who is to lead the disciples of Jesus into all

the truth. And while the old light will not be quenched, but made incomparably brighter by the new illumination, it is conceivable that new revelations may compel us to discard some of the old forms and formulas, old polities and dogmas, and construct new. "The Holy Spirit," writes Professor Herrmann, "works synthetically, not analytically, and the composition of the New Testament clearly shows this. If Christians seek unity by means of unalterable doctrine, then they must give up the authority of the New Testament. For in the New Testament there is no unalterable doctrine which embraces the whole scheme of Christian thought. . . . It is no imperfection, it is rather an excellence, and thoroughly as it should be, that the epistles of the New Testament are messages for definite circumstances, and not contributions to a doctrinal system which shall be valid to all eternity."[1]

Favorable to the cultivation of such a spirit of fellowship as is essential to the fullest unity of the Church, is the clearer recognition of the measure of unity that already prevails among Christians. Members of a single denomination constitute a community that is bound together by all they jointly possess. There is a sense of likeness, a unanimity of thought, among its constituents; a realization of group individuality that arises from

[1] *Communion with God*, p. 9.

participation in the same convictions and activities, and in the same memories and hopes.
This group individuality rests in a sense of the
continuity of the past, now stored in memory, and
of the future, now conceived in terms of hope and
expectation, with the present, all within a single
consciousness. Such a condition of oneness characterizes every separate body of Christian people.
Similarly all Christian churches are bound together
in a larger and more inclusive individuality, sharing
with one another a vast fund of Christian truth more
fundamental than their differences, and the memories, hopes, and expectations that belong to Christians of every name. There is a "communion of the
saints" that is very real in spite of all differences
among them. There is a "Holy Catholic Church"
that transcends all artificial boundaries, whose uni-
fying elements are a common vital energy, a general
history, and a mutual ambition for the future. How
rich is the heritage of this community, how vigor-
ous this interpenetrating life, and how harmonious
its aims! And the strongest of all the bonds that
unite those that enter into it is loyalty to one Lord
and Saviour, Jesus Christ. The same sun shines
in London and in New York: it is not the same
sunshine, but it is the same sun; and every eye that
gazes upon it, and every frame that feels its warmth, is
thereby united with every other over the whole earth.

There is a unity of Christian scholarship that ignores denominational divisions and seeks only the truth—the whole truth. "The lovers of the truth are one." The modern Revised Bible in English, as Dr. Schaff has pointed out, is a noble monument to a united Christian scholarship, representing, as it does, the harmonious labors, through fourteen years, of about one hundred British and American scholars of various affiliations—Episcopalians, Independents, Presbyterians, Methodists, Baptists, Friends, and Unitarians.

There is already a degree of doctrinal unity among the great evangelical bodies of Christendom. Differ as they may in dogma and theology, they agree in the fundamental articles of faith that are necessary to salvation. All believe in the one Father in heaven, in the one Lord and Saviour, Jesus Christ, all accept the same Bible, and can repeat together the Apostles' Creed. There is also a devotional unity: all worship the same God, revealed in Christ; all pray together in the words taught them by their Master, and surround the same throne of grace. In sacred song they unite hearts and voices in the great hymns of the Church universal, by whomsoever they may have been written, whether it be "Rock of Ages," by Toplady, the Calvinist; or "Jesus, Lover of My Soul," by Wesley, the Methodist; or "In the Cross of Christ I Glory," by Bowring, the Unitarian; or

"Hark! hark, my soul!" by Faber, the Roman Catholic.

There is also an ethical unity. All revere the same qualities of Christian character, though they may arrange them in different orders of precedence. All cultivate the fruit of the Spirit as defined by the apostle, and acknowledge Jesus as the model Man. All accept the Ten Commandments as interpreted by Jesus and believe the whole law to be fulfilled in love to God and neighbor. Books on Christian ethics are not dependent for their value upon the denominational creed of their authors, but upon the fidelity with which they represent the spirit and teaching of Jesus and reflect the contents of the Christian consciousness.

There is unity, moreover, in the forms of activity to which Christian charity incites. "Mrs. Barbauld"—I quote from James Freeman Clarke—"has a little apologue to show that charity, or love to man, is the same thing in all sects and churches. A mother is walking with her little boy on Sunday in the streets of a large city. The street is filled with people who turn into different churches,—some into the Established Church, some into the different chapels. And the little boy wonders why, since they have the same Master, they should go in such different directions. But when the services are over, and the people are on their way home, a man falls in the street with a sudden attack of illness; and then a Presbyterian runs and lifts him from the ground, a Methodist runs for a doctor, a Baptist gets water and bathes his forehead; and the mother, turning to her little boy, says, 'You see, my child, that though their modes of worship are different, their charity is the same.'" Men separate for their *services* but unite for *service*.

Finally, there is unity in the conception of the fundamental aim and purpose of the Church that is held by all branches of it. All would agree that the function of the Church is the establishment upon earth of the kingdom of God, defined as the rule of God in the hearts of men. A social state in which all men live as children of the Father in heaven, and brethren one of another, is the dream that all communions cherish in common. Differ as they may, the united desire of all the churches is to infuse into men the spirit of the Christ until it transforms all hearts, transfigures all human institutions, and redeems man and society. Not in the fact that "we are all trying to get to the same place hereafter," as is so often fatuously said, but in the fact that we are all living together in the same place here, and that it is not now a satisfactory place to live in, lies the basis for unity of program and action for the Church. Men may conceive that separate heavens will be provided hereafter, but there is no question that the fates of men are bound up together here where

> "Rich men hate the poor, who curse the rich,
>   Who agonize together, rich and poor,
>   Over and under in the social spasm
>   And crisis of the ages."

There is very general agreement that if the world is to be made over into the kingdom of God, it must be by all men of good-will working together.

Such a conception of the mission of the Church forms the basis of a union immediately possible, and suggests the means by which a unity still more complete may be achieved. Union of effort for the accomplishment of the practical program of the Church may not only be undertaken at once, but will open the way for other forms of co-operation and federation hardly conceivable at present. Absolutely nothing counts in Christendom but Christlikeness: that alone is essence; the remainder is accident. When Christians thoroughly appreciate this and accept it with all its consequences, they will be willing to agree also that all that helps the development of Christlikeness in men and nations should be approved and accepted, and that that which is discovered to advance it most should be adopted by all. In proportion as the efforts of Christian men the world over are directed, not to

the building up of particular institutions, at the
expense, it may be, of others, or to the formulation
of creeds, but to doing the things that Jesus came
to do, to lifting up the lives of men, in that proportion denominational differences will sink into insignificance as unworthy the place they have occupied in modern thought. "All classes of Christians," said David Livingstone, "find that sectarian
rancor soon dies out when they are working together for the real heathen."

Here, at least, is a platform upon which all Christians can meet. We do not need to wait until we
worship together before we labor as one. There is
nothing that so promotes mutual acquaintance,
understanding, and esteem as co-operation in a common task. Said the head of a great industry, after
some months of work upon the board of directors of
a philanthropic society among whom were some of his
own workmen, "These workingmen are a fine lot:
it is a pleasure to know them. When they come
to me in future to discuss some matter of work and
wages I shall feel quite differently about it, now that
we have become really acquainted." Union in
unselfish service is the shortest road to fellowship.
In so far as Christian men labor together to alleviate
poverty, to protect the life of youth, to heal the sick,
and to minister to all the needs of men, they will
find themselves knit together by bonds of sympathy

so close that no differences in creed will be permitted to break them, and the way will be opened for co-operation in every form of service in which the Church can engage, and for fellowship in worship. The federation of Christian forces in the field of social service is the first step in the direction of organic unity. If such federation is impossible, it is futile to hope for something closer and more exacting still. Programs of church unity that begin with the attempt to secure agreement in doctrine and polity, and that have no patience for the slower processes of education through co-operation in practical tasks, are doomed to failure. Mutual acquaintance, understanding, and esteem must precede any form of corporate unity, and these are secured best through co-operation in specific endeavors.

The influences making to-day for a better understanding among the churches are many, the points of attachment are multiplying every year; but the process of the unification of Christendom will not progress faster than does the increase of love. Denominations, like metals, fuse only when at white heat. There is a story of certain bridge-builders who were engaged in constructing the two halves of the single arch that was to span a river. From either side of the river they labored simultaneously, building out from the great piers on opposite banks the two arms of the bridge that were to meet in the middle. The day came when, at nightfall, the last truss and girder were put into place, but to their dismay the plates of the bridge were several inches apart and would not meet. But the next morning the sun rose above the horizon and, as it neared the zenith, poured its warm rays upon all below; and the foreman, walking out upon the bridge, found that the two great arms of the arch had expanded until they touched each other and were easily riveted together. While coldness of heart drives us apart, the warmth of Christian love thus draws us together. The greatest hindrance to unity is lack of the Christ spirit. Selfishness is always divisive. "I didn't get that family to come to us," a good woman was heard to say, "but one thing is certain, —they will never go to the other church!" Such a spirit would delay the unity of the Church until the day of judgment! But when the churches are possessed of the spirit of John the Baptist, when he said of his Master, "He must increase, but I must decrease," essential Church unity is already achieved.

Such a spirit of sacrifice is contagious: it spreads from heart to heart. "As in water face answereth to face, so the heart of man to man." The cause of Christian unity waits for the church that shall first have the courage to lose its life for Christ's sake and the gospel's; and if this spirit be there, such a church,

7

according to the promise, far from losing its life, will find it unto life eternal. When all churches shall be willing thus to lose, all shall gain, and the cause of the Kingdom will go forward with leaps and bounds. There is a legend in the Talmud of two brothers who owned in common a field upon the site on which King Solomon later built the first Temple at Jerusalem. One night, so the story runs, the younger of the brothers said, "My brother has a wife and children to support, while I have no one to care for but myself. I will go into the harvest field and take some of the sheaves of grain that fall to me and put them with my brother's sheaves without his knowledge, that he may have sufficient to provide for those he loves." On the same night the other thought, "God has blessed me with wife and children, while my brother lives alone. I will arise and take of my shocks of grain and lay them with my brother's share that he may be comforted in his loneliness." Thus, in the morning, to their surprise, each found his share undiminished. The next night each repeated his kind deed and with the same result. On the third night both brothers determined to watch, and, to their mutual surprise, they met in the middle of the field, each laden with his golden sheaves. And God said of the spot where they embraced, "This is the holiest spot I know: here I will build my holy Temple."

The cultivation of such a spirit of love ought to be possible within the Church, for love is the essence of religion. Religion is social comradeship. It has, indeed, been said that, as a matter of fact, religion has exercised a divisive influence in history and has served to keep men apart. So a superficial reading of history might seem to indicate. But below the surface differences which it has evoked, religion has been the fundamental bond that has held humanity together through centuries of evolution, the living principle that has made of society an organism. "It would be impossible," writes Benjamin Kidd, "to conceive any economic or political motive influencing the human mind so consistently or continuously, and on so large a scale, and producing over so prolonged a period results of such character and magnitude as that of religion. It has been said of the synthetic philosophy that Spencer found little place in it for systems of religion except in relation to our emancipation from the past. But no change which is in progress in our time as the result of the extending conception of society is more striking than that which is taking place in our estimate of the influences in the evolution of society of the integrating conceptions of the human mind hitherto represented mainly in the great systems of religion, which are thus in the deepest sense rendering society organic. It would seem as if it is these

stones which the builders of social science in the past
have rejected that we must place now as the head-
stones of the corners."[1]   Religion is the vital principle of spiritual evolution, and religion without
love ceases to be religious.   The "spirit of Christian
unity" is the spirit of love, and it is futile to imagine
that the unification of Christendom will ever be
consummated by any scheme of organization of
which Christian love is not the organizing principle.
"Beloved, let us love one another: for love is of God."

[1] *Individualism and After*, p. 27.

CHRISTIAN UNITY THROUGH FEDERATION

Unity best promoted by effort.—Increase in organization.—
The Federal Council of Churches of Christ in America.—
Work of the Commission on Social Service; on Home and
Foreign Missions.—Local, State, and City Federations.—
Duplication avoided.—A plan for co-operation in a city.—
Relation of the Church to such federations.

CHAPTER V

THE unity of the Church will never be *thought out* until it has been *worked out*. "Union will not come," said a missionary in China in discussing the problem upon the missionary field, "simply by good-will, or by doctrinal adroitness to bring it about. It will come by those who unitedly love the Lord and who wish to serve him, working together." The results of the repeated attempts that have been made to secure agreement in matters of faith and order among the divided bodies of Christendom have not thus far proved very encouraging, while the results of endeavors through co-operation in all forms of Christian effort in which co-operation can be secured, to reach the degree of practical unity which is already possible, are beginning to transform the Christian world, and are fostering that spirit of mutual appreciation and that common understanding which are essential to the achievement of any form of union more ideal. It is becoming increasingly evident that the latter is the hopeful and logical order of procedure. Let the churches that now find it difficult to worship together unite in some great moral crusade, —for the eradication of white slavery, or for the restriction of the evils of the liquor traffic. Let the churches that can worship together, but that cannot commune together; that can commune together, but cannot dismiss members one to the other, or acknowledge the validity of one another's administration of the ordinances, organize union evangelistic compaigns, and pray much together. If the members of the various churches unite in labor and in prayer, we need not fear but that they will learn to love one another better and to see more clearly eye to eye; and they will find a way for a closer and ever closer union. The Apostle Paul bade the Ephesian Christians endeavor "to keep the unity of the Spirit in the bond of peace" until a doctrinal unity, sure to flow from it, should be possible,—"till we all attain unto the unity of the faith, and of the knowledge of the Son of God."[1]

The last decade has seen a remarkable crystallization of the sentiment of Christian unity in the organization of various forms of associations, national, state, and local, through which American Protestantism may co-operate in common tasks. Foremost among these is the Federal Council of Churches of Christ in America, which was organized in 1905. Its growth in influence and usefulness since its organization has been steadily advancing, until it includes at the present date 29 constituent bodies,

[1] Eph. 4 : 3, 13 ff.

to which should be added the Protestant Episcopal Church, which is affiliated through its Commissions on Christian Unity and Social Service. These denominations thus united for service contain a total of over 138,000 churches with almost 17,000,000 communicants, and include practically all the larger Protestant bodies. The purpose of the Council is well indicated in the preamble to its Constitution, which states: "In the providence of God the time has come when it seems fitting more fully to manifest the essential oneness of the Christian churches of America in Jesus Christ as their divine Lord and Saviour, and to promote the spirit of fellowship, service, and co-operation among them." The limitations of its functions are specifically stated in the constitutional provision that "The Federal Council shall have no authority over the constituent bodies adhering to it; but its province shall be limited to the expression of its counsel and the recommending of a course of action in matters of common interest to the churches, local councils, and individual Christians. It has no authority to draw up a common creed, or form of government or worship; or in any way to limit the full autonomy of the Christian churches adhering to it." Yet under these limitations the influence it has exerted upon its constituent bodies and upon public opinion at large has been a steadily increasing factor in the religious and moral

life of the country. Through it the united voice of
Protestantism has been heard for the first time in
America, upon the great moral questions that concern the welfare of all the people. Various practical
undertakings have been successfully prosecuted,
such as no single denomination could have accomplished alone, and great causes have felt behind
them, through its activities, the united force of the
churches. Through the Federal Council, which
meets quadrennially and which consists of about
400 qualified delegates, the degree of unity that
already exists has been impressively exhibited, and
the movement toward a still more effective union
has been greatly stimulated. The scope of the work
of the Council is indicated by the names of the Commissions through which it is accomplished, which are
as follows: State and Local Federations, Foreign
Missions, Home Missions, Religious Education,
Social Service, Evangelism, Family Life, Sunday
Observance, Temperance, and Peace and Arbitration. Three of these Commissions,—those on Peace
and Arbitration, Evangelism, and Social Service,—
employ executive secretaries in the direction of their
work. The general work of the Council is conducted
by a secretary, the Rev. Charles S. Macfarland, with
an office in New York, and an associate secretary,
the Rev. Henry K. Carroll, with an office in Washington.

It is natural that thus far the work of the Commission on Social Service should have been the most largely developed and fruitful. In this field all the constituent denominations, however varied their ecclesiastical polity and creedal statements, find a platform upon which they may stand and labor together. At the quadrennial meeting in Chicago in 1913 the Council adopted as its social creed a comprehensive statement so admirable and so far-reaching in its outlook that it will furnish for the Christian forces of America a program of social service that will suffice for years to come. The Council affirmed that the Churches must stand:

1. For equal rights and complete justice for all men in all stations of life.

2. For the protection of the family, by the single standard of purity, uniform divorce laws, proper regulation of marriage, and proper housing.

3. For the fullest possible development for every child, especially by the provision of proper education and recreation.

4. For the abolition of child labor.

5. For such regulation of the conditions of toil for women as shall safeguard the physical and moral health of the community.

6. For the abatement and prevention of poverty.

7. For the protection of the individual and society from the social, economic, and moral waste of the liquor traffic.

8. For the conservation of health.

9. For the protection of the worker from dangerous machinery, occupational diseases and mortality.

10. For the right of all men to the opportunity for self-maintenance, for safeguarding this right against encroachments of every kind, and for the protection of workers from the hardships of enforced unemployment.

11. For suitable provision for the old age of the workers, and for those incapacitated by injury.

12. For the right of employees and employers alike to organize for adequate means of conciliation and arbitration in industrial disputes.

13. For a release from employment one day in seven.

14. For the gradual and reasonable reduction of the hours of labor to the lowest practicable point, and for that degree of leisure for all which is a condition of the highest human life.

15. For a living wage as a minimum in every industry, and for the highest wage that each industry can afford.

16. For a new emphasis upon the application of Christian principles to the acquisition and use of property, and for the most equitable division of the product of industry that can ultimately be devised.

If the Council had done no more than to secure the acceptance on the part of the accredited representatives of the great Protestant army of a social program so definite, constructive, and vital as this, it would have abundantly justified its existence. Protestant Christianity in America has long been accused of indifference toward the social movement, and to this apathy has been ascribed the alienation of the workingman from all forms of organized religion. As the churches apply themselves seriously to the task of Christianizing the world of industry, such a reproach, in so far as it has been true, will be taken away. It is a great step gained that there should be set before them for their guidance such a statement of duty as this to which the Christian conscience of America can subscribe.

The Commissions on Home Missions and Foreign Missions are in close co-operation with the Home Missions and Foreign Missions Councils, organizations of representatives of the various denominational societies or boards responsible for the conduct of missionary work. Through the Commission on Peace and Arbitration, the federated churches have both spoken and labored in the interest of worldwide peace with a force that has attracted the attention of the entire country. Lately, special efforts have been made by the Executive Committee of the Council to safeguard the moral and religious interests of the thousands of American soldiers and sailors. More recently the work of the Council has assumed an international aspect in the appointment, at the earnest solicitation of missionaries in Japan, of a Commission on Relations with Japan for the purpose of sending "an ambassador of the churches to convey a message to the Japanese people, or the Eastern peoples in general, from the Federal Council, as representing the Christian sentiment of America," and of extending "an invitation to some representative of the Japanese people to come to this country

for the same purpose." The first half of this object
has since been achieved in the visit to Japan, early
in 1915, of Dr. Shailer Mathews, President of the
Federal Council, and Prof. Sidney L. Gulick, as the
accredited representatives of American Protestant
Christianity. The cordial welcome given them, not
only by the churches of Japan, but by the highest
representatives of the government, local and
national, made it possible for them to render a
service of great value to the cause of international
friendship, and to contribute to a better understanding between the two countries. The appointment of this Commission "to study the entire
question of the application of the teachings of Christ
to our relations with Japan, and to promote such
influences and activities as shall lead to the right
relationships between the peoples of these two
nations," marks the entrance of the Federal Council into a new and larger sphere of usefulness. The
Council has now under advisement, also, the question of the calling of a World Congress to consider
international relations from a Christian stand-
point.

The latest expression of the desire of the Federal
Council to promote the co-operative spirit is found
in its proposal of the creation of a new "Commission
on Federated Movements." For the promotion of
the work of such a Commission, the Council lately

appointed the Rev. Roy B. Guild as associate secretary. The purpose of the proposed Commission is indicated in the results of the Conference held, by invitation of the Council, at Atlantic City in June, 1915, when about one hundred leaders of denominational and interdenominational organizations met to formulate a plan under which the agencies they represent might be brought into harmonious co-operation. Among the eighteen organizations represented were the Federal Council, the International Sunday-School Association, the Missionary Education Movement, the Young Men's and Young Women's Christian Associations, the Laymen's Missionary Movement, the Home Missions Council, the Christian Endeavor Society, and various denominational young people's societies and brotherhoods. These organizations have been conducting their campaigns, for the most part, independently of one another, with consequent confusion, conflict of dates, and unwise multiplication of appeals to the churches. In accordance with the recommendations of this Conference, the Federal Council will appoint the "Commission on Federated Movements," choosing its members "from persons eminently identified with interdenominational and undenominational religious organizations," and "from persons who have had characteristic experience in state and local city church federations."

While the Commission will have a purely advisory and unofficial relation to the organizations in whose interest it is formed, it will be in a position, through the cordial co-operation on their part, which appears to be already assured, to render a valuable and necessary service in the co-ordination of their activities. Its special field will be the study of the history and present status of federative organizations of all types, national, state, and local,—to determine the most effective methods of church co-operation, and in what spheres it is immediately most possible,— the fostering of existing city federations, and the forming of such federations where they are needed.

The formation of local federations of churches preceded the foundation of the Federal Council, but the latter has greatly stimulated such local manifestations of the spirit of co-operation throughout the land. At the last report[1] there were about 150 such federations in the country, of which 21 were state organizations; but the movement spreads so rapidly that statistics need continual revision. County federations, particularly in country districts, are furthering community surveys, and inaugurating forms of co-operation for the solution of the problems that they disclose. State federations, under various names, some of

---

[1] Compiled under the direction of the Commission on State and Local Federations in 1914.

them with executive secretaries giving their entire time to the work of the organization, are fostering co-operative effort in city, town, and country, and are seeking to minimize the effects of over-churching and to care for neglected districts wherever discovered. Intensive studies of wide areas of the country have been made by state federations, and the spirit of denominational comity, which they express, is gradually transforming the competitive spirit into one of cordial fellowship in service.

Chaotic conditions of religious activity in the larger cities are slowly giving way, where effective federations under competent leadership have been organized, before the advance of a new program of a united campaign for righteousness. The city gives little heed to a single voice, however powerful it may be, when raised in protest against some flagrant evil; nor is it greatly stirred when an entire denomination unites in protest; but when churches of every name join forces and speak together, the whole city listens and the powers of evil tremble. Organized vice knows no divisive creeds: the saloon in politics is neither Baptist nor Methodist. The forces of evil know how to sink their differences in times of stress, and at the first sound of battle they unite for defense. The churches cannot postpone practical co-operation until their differences are composed, so long as problems of social justice cry for

8

solution, and vice flaunts itself unrebuked, and a conspiracy of evil claims our sons and daughters, and corrupt political forces threaten the foundations of democracy itself. The churches have already learned that they can trust one another sufficiently to unite to labor for law-enforcement and the enthronement of justice and righteousness in social life; and with every successful attempt to work together in such enterprises there is secured added confidence and courage.

The strength of such union is evident not merely in protest and suppression; it is more effective still in the promotion of practical measures for the accomplishment of the positive tasks of the Church. Through practical co-operation in action, the churches are discovering that in the essential things they already stand together and that they can work in Christian love for many ends without loss or sacrifice to any. A new conception of the interdependence of the churches is appearing. As in the federated unity of the body which Paul describes, "Whether one member suffereth, all the members suffer with it; or one member is honored, all the members rejoice with it," so what harms a single church in the community injures all the churches; and any accession of strength to any church inures to the benefit of the rest. So long as the function of the Church was conceived to be exclusively remedial, and the numerical addition of adherents was the sole test of its success, there may have been some excuse for envy and competition; but if it is also the function of the Church to create an atmosphere wherein purity and integrity and unselfishness may flourish, and in which vice shall wither and die, then the larger the contribution of a single church to the result, the more the churches at large will profit.

The task of the modern city church is so exacting, and the failure of any single communion to cope in any adequate manner with the problems that press upon it in crowded centers is so apparent, that the necessity of united effort is imperative. To endure the waste of competition and of "overlapping," and the neglect of opportunity and duty through "overlooking" that is consequent upon it, is disloyal to the Lord of the Church. In the face of the need of the world, the luxury of isolation is maintained at an unwarrantable expense. We are merely scratching the surface of opportunity in the larger cities. The dense masses of foreign-speaking peoples have hardly been touched by Protestant influences. The task of instilling American and Christian ideals into the immigrant population must not be left to the Roman Catholic Church: Protestantism also is obliged to make its contribution. And it is worse than folly, when the task and the opportunity are so large and pressing, for individual churches or denominations to enter the field without consultation with one another, or understanding what others are attempting. If a division of the foreign mission field into spheres of responsibility and influence is needed, such a division is as clearly necessary in all unoccupied fields in the home land. In many instances, efforts for the evangelization of foreign-speaking peoples may be undertaken by various denominations working together, with a far better prospect of success than would attend the work of a single denomination. If it is unwise to carry the *minutiæ* of our denominational differences into China, is it wise to inflict them upon the Chinese in America?

It is a hopeful sign of a new day that five denominations are co-operating in the support and direction of the First Chinese Evangelical Church of Chicago. In 1911 there was organized upon the Pacific Coast the Oriental Workers' Association, to labor among the Chinese, Japanese, and Koreans, including, within its membership, Baptists, Methodists, Disciples, Congregationalists, Presbyterians, Cumberland Presbyterians, Episcopalians, and Friends. One of the first results of the work of the Standing Committee was the transfer, with the cordial approval of both the denominations interested, of a mission from the Congregationalists to the Presbyterians, the former having no American church in the city in which the mission was located. The entire enterprise of city missions is an inviting field for interdenominational co-operation, as is illustrated by the activities of the Chicago Co-operative Council of City Missions which has recently been established to further the following aims: the evangelization of the foreign population of the city, the maintenance of churches in the central portion of the city, and the establishment of new churches in the residential sections.

It is a function of church federation not merely to unite the churches, but to separate them, to extricate them from the entanglements and embarrassments incident to the competitive method, or lack of method, that has prevailed in the past. A vast amount of duplicative work may be avoided through the assignment to each federated church of a particular district or parish for which it shall accept responsibility. Under such a plan an entire city may be included in such areas of responsibility, each church being assigned a district within easy reach of its own building and, where necessary, a supplementary district at a distance. If each church will then canvass its district and maintain a directory, constantly revised, that will account for the denominational preference and church attendance of each individual within it, caring itself for the unattached and indifferent, and assigning to churches of their own faith all who express a particular denominational preference, such a plan will go far to solve the problem both of "overlapping" and "overlooking" within the city. When the Church knows the people within its district as intimately as the politician knows the voters in his ward or precinct, it will be better able to serve and to win them. System saves time and strength and makes for increased efficiency at a lower cost. Haphazard methods are as inadequate in religion as in business. Such a plan makes it possible for each church to conduct an intensive survey of its district, and to acquaint itself with the moral conditions and needs of the people who dwell within it, and thus to render a more intelligent and helpful ministry. If a moral reform needs to be inaugurated within the district, here is the instrument ready to accomplish it. A diffused and general ministry that extends in about equal proportions over an entire city is not likely to be so effective for good as such a specialized ministry to a particular district thus thoroughly understood. Under such a plan, also, each church represents all the churches and is responsible to all the churches for the administration of the district which it has accepted, and feels behind it the power of the united Christian forces of the city and the encouragement of that added community respect that always results when denominations are found working together in such actual unity.

The opportunities for co-operation through federation are almost without limit, though the direction it takes in particular localities is determined by local needs and circumstances. Christian education is a fruitful field for united action, as is the promotion of missionary instruction and interest and, to a somewhat narrower extent, evangelistic effort. But the field within which the churches can combine with the least probability of friction is that of constructive social service. Through federation the churches may make a united impression upon the community in the interest of every movement that strives for human betterment, and furnish substantial aid to every program of reform. The churches when federated may initiate and influence the course of legislation as single churches cannot, and may be rallied to the support of charities and philanthropies, to the cause of juvenile protection, public playgrounds, and social centers; thus federated Christianity may lead all the forces that labor for the welfare of humanity.

It has been said that such federal union is opportunism in religion, and it is probably true. It takes the half loaf that is immediately available and makes the most of it. It asks for no compromise of principle or surrender of ecclesiastical claims on the part of the churches that enter it, nor does it seek to commit any one of its constituent churches to co-operation in any enterprise undertaken by the federation where such co-operation appears inexpedient or impossible. Any church is free to withdraw from such a federation at its pleasure, or to withhold co-operation in particular instances while retaining its membership.

State federations are, like the Federal Council, associations of denominations, while county and city federations may be composed either of delegates from denominations or from individual churches. There is, however, no formal or official connection between the Federal Council and the state federations, or between those of states and the local federations within the states. Church Federation is a general name for groups of churches variously organized, and stands for the loosest, freest form of co-operative union possible in which efficiency, in the particular kinds of activity contemplated, can be preserved. Its strength lies in its weakness, as the bond of love and fellowship, and the friendship that springs from working together for practical ends are stronger than the compulsion of ecclesiastical authority. Such a form of co-operation has decided limitations: it is not claimed for it that it is the ideal form of Christian unity. It was forced upon the churches by the immediate necessity of facing with a united front their common problems and tasks, because it was the best form and method immediately possible. To have waited for the adjustment of ecclesiastical and theological differences, and for the attainment of organic unity, before attempting such tasks would have been to subject the cause of the kingdom of God to irreparable loss.

Imperfect and incomplete as are all such forms of federal union, they are rendering, wherever there is forceful leadership, a splendid service. Notable results have been accomplished in many communities. It is no light thing that the churches should have discovered that they can labor and pray together, and speak, on occasion, with a single voice. Experiments in federation have drawn the churches together and have disclosed the measure of unity that they already possess, and, by promoting the spirit of Christian love, have pointed out the direction from which must come any hopeful plan of closer fellowship. Religion is a life of love: theology is a philosophy. Religion dwells in the heart: theology is of the head; and the foundation of unity lies below the level at which we do our thinking.

THE UNION OF CHRISTIAN
FORCES IN COUNTRY
AND VILLAGE

Increasing interest in social, economic, and religious aspects of rural life.—Decline of the country church.—Rural conditions under special investigation.—Possibilities and responsibilities of the rural church.—Over-churched conditions.—Statistics concerning church competition in rural communities.—Further facts from Board of Home Missions of the Presbyterian Church (North).—Examples from New York and Vermont.—Three forms of federation proposed and discussed: church federation, the federated church, the union denominational church.

CHAPTER VI

THE UNION OF CHRISTIAN FORCES IN COUNTRY AND VILLAGE

AMONG the signs of the times none is more encouraging than the awakening of a new sense of the importance of, and a new interest in the success of, the rural church. Through the report of the Commission on Country Life, appointed by President Roosevelt, the attention of the entire country was called to a fresh consideration of the problems and possibilities of rural life. A new literature has suddenly sprung into existence dealing with its social, economic, and religious aspects, the effects of which may already be seen in the rise of a more intelligent social consciousness in many a village and hamlet, and in an increase of self-respect on the part of many a community. The facts are rapidly being gathered that will form the basis of plans and programs for the fuller development of the rich resources of country life. Surveys and intensive studies of particular communities reveal that the conditions which prevail are not peculiar to any single section, but that the problem is largely the same throughout the length and breadth of the land.

Among the facts which have been brought to light, however, is that of the gradual decline of the country church. A wide-spread indifference to the Church is prevalent everywhere in rural communities. The percentage of the community attendant upon the services of the Church is less, in general, than ten or twenty years ago, and is still decreasing; nor is the membership holding its own in proportion to the population. The average salary of the country minister, always lamentably inadequate, while it has somewhat increased in the gross during the last score of years, is, as we have already seen, actually less in proportion to the increase in the cost of living than at the beginning of the period. Among the ministers who serve country parishes are to be found many of the most intelligent, the noblest, and most unselfish within the profession; but the proportion of those who possess the measure of training adequate to meet the exacting conditions under which the modern minister must do his work, when the level of general enlightenment has so greatly risen, has not increased. Discouragement and apathy are reported from many quarters. The spectacle of churches deserted, closed, and sold at auction is not uncommon. The church, once the center of community life, the one institution around which the varied interests of the neighborhood were organized, has become too often the occasion of discord and division. With, happily, multitudes of churches exceptional enough to prove a rule, the church of the village and rural districts does not hold to-day the place in the affections and loyalty of the group to which it seeks to minister that it has held in the past.

To the problems that such facts as these suggest there has been brought in recent years the intelligent consideration of a multitude of earnest men. The field has been surveyed and the results of study have been widely published. A growing literature is being created. Conferences of leaders in country life are becoming frequent. Great universities that minister to a country constituency have established departments under skilled leadership which are devoting themselves to the study of conditions, and to the dissemination of information and practical suggestions that are leading to the development of the latent resources of rural life. The period of analysis is drawing to a close and the adoption of certain positive and constructive principles is becoming apparent.

In so far as these concern the Church it is becoming evident that the rural church possesses the key to the situation, occupying a place of vantage from which it can do more than any other institution to enrich and deepen the life of the community, and that, if it is to fulfil its mission and rise to its

opportunity, the outlook, and spirit, and method of
the church must be changed to accord with the needs
of the new order. The rural church must get closer
to the soil, must serve the community at more
points than heretofore, recognizing with a greater
sympathetic discernment the actual interests of
those whom it would reach, and minister to these
with a wider intelligence and a more unselfish
devotion. Once more the country church must
become the community center, organizing about
itself as many as possible of the interests of the social
group in which it is set, now so much more diverse
and complex than formerly. This is even more
incumbent upon the church of the open country
than upon that of the town or city where social and
intellectual opportunities are so much more abundant. Unrest and discontent in village and hamlet
spring from hungers unsatisfied and legitimate
impulses denied expression, and the impoverishment of life that such deprivations involve; and
never was there a time when larger possibilities and
a more inspiring mission summoned the rural
church to a life of service.

The unanimous testimony of those who are bringing their experience and intelligence to bear upon
the solution of the problem that confronts the
church in the country is that the chief obstacle to
the achievement of its noblest possibilities is the

overlapping and competition consequent upon the unnecessary multiplication of separate organizations. "Examples like that of the town in Pennsylvania in which, within a four-mile drive of a given point in the open country," writes Warren H. Wilson, "are twenty-four country churches, are numerous in all parts of the country. . . . In a Michigan group of villages, the whole population of which is seventeen hundred, there are fifteen country churches in which thirteen resident ministers are at work." In many a village, whose population is barely sufficient for the support of a single church, there may be seen around the village green a group of churches, three or four in number, standing as silent witnesses to the folly of denominational rivalry. Years ago, perhaps, they were established by denominational agencies eager to multiply adherents at a time when the community gave promise of a growth not subsequently realized. Now, with buildings erected, and constituencies gathered, and local loyalties created, and sectarian convictions carefully cultivated, it is difficult either to advance or to retreat. A sense of denominational responsibility to the group of worshipers that has been gathered under the tacit promise of missionary aid sometimes appears to forbid withdrawal. Occasionally a denomination in the field feels so strongly the vital importance of the peculiar truths for which it

9

stands as conscientiously to believe that its witness should be continued at any cost of men and money. Sometimes it is denominational pride alone that holds the fort. Progress is forbidden by the very nature of the circumstances. In a constituency so limited no church can advance except at the expense of another. The division of the religious forces of the community is so minute that every church is poor, engaged in a perpetual struggle to keep the wolf from the ecclesiastical door. Thus they stand, three or four churches where one would suffice, a waste of ministerial service, a reduplication of equipments involving unnecessary expense of many kinds, dividing the available total of religious energy; and the results are what might be expected: poverty drives the churches to resort to unworthy methods of money-raising; salaries are so small that only the less effective sort of ministers can be secured; competition between churches breeds prejudice and division; denominational peculiarities are exaggerated in the very effort of particular churches to provide an excuse for their existence; and gradually the Church as an institution loses the respect and the support of a large proportion of the people and is deposed from leadership in the life of the community.

That a church chances to be the only church in a community is no guarantee of its success: that will

depend upon efficient leadership. There is, moreover, an emulation in good works between churches
in the same neighborhood that is wholesome and
stimulating under many circumstances. However,
it cannot be gainsaid that wherever the number of
churches in proportion to the population is such
that they struggle with one another for existence,
the gain of one being dependent upon the loss of
another, the spirit of Christian love, which is the
essence of Christianity, is sure to suffer strain and
rupture. While they do not compete with the same
degree of acrimony, the fate of such churches is
likely to be similar to that of the Kilkenny cats, of
whom it will be remembered that at the end of the
struggle "instead of two cats there weren't any."

The consensus of opinion is rapidly coming to be
that the religious needs of communities of less than
one thousand population are most efficiently served
by a single township church, unless the people are
scattered over a very large area. Even the needs
of thinly settled outlying districts may often best
be met by establishing preaching stations around a
single church center. The cost in both money and
members of the maintenance of several churches,
where one church is sufficient to minister to the needs
of the entire population, is convincingly shown in the
following statistics gathered by the Massachusetts
Federation of Churches in 1907 from a study of the

one hundred most sparsely populated towns of the
state, ten towns being included in each of the
groups considered:

	Average population.	Members.	Income.	Home Mission Aid.	Salary.
Towns with one church.	725	110	$1102	$15	$874
Towns with two churches					
(Church)		71.4	781	25	687
(Town)..............	724	143	1562	50	
Towns with three churches					
(Church)		51	492	52	473
(Town).............	725	154	1477	155	

These figures indicate, as the Rev. E. Tallmadge
Root, Secretary of the Federation, points out, that
where churches are multiplied in such communities
as these, not only is the efficiency of the individual
churches lessened, but the total cost of church
maintenance increases at a rate more rapid than
that of the increase of churches. The salaries of
ministers, small at the best, decrease, on the other
hand, with each increase in the number of churches,
from an average of $874 in the one-church town to
$687 in the two-church town and to $473 in the three-
church town. While the percentage of the population within the membership of the churches increases from 15.17 per cent. in the first class to
19.75 per cent. in the second and 21.24 per cent.
in the third, the increase is sadly disproportionate

to the number of churches at work and to the cost
per town. For, as Mr. Root says, "It is apparent
that while the membership is increased 30 per cent.
by duplicating, and 40 per cent. by tripling the
churches, the cost per town, including Home Missionary aid, increases 44 per cent. and 47 per cent.
respectively, while the amount of aid called for per
town is $3\frac{1}{2}$ and 10 times as much!" The decrease
in the average number of members to each church
as the number of churches in the towns increases,
from 110 in one-church to 71.4 in two-church and
51 in three-church towns, may fairly be taken as an
indication of the degree of competition between the
churches which results from their multiplication.
If the churches, in other words, drew from the un-
churched population, and not from one another, the
average membership would be the same whether
there were one, two, or three churches in the town.
"To place a second church by the side of the first,"
comments Mr. Root, "increases the total membership by only 33; i. e., of the 143 members, 110 would
have been secured by a single church. Does not
this mean that nearly 77 per cent. of the energy of
both churches is spent in competition? To add a
third church wins 11 more, and the same calcula-
tion indicates that almost 93 per cent. of effort must
be competitive. What if a fourth be added? In
the three smallest four-church towns, with an aver-

age population of 786 instead of 725, the average
church membership is but 33, and the total for the
town is only 141; which would seem to show, as we
might expect, that the competition becomes so in-
tense and costly that four churches actually win a
smaller proportion than two would do."

This aspect of the situation suggests another unfortunate result of the unwise reduplication of
churches in small communities. More significant
even than the unnecessary cost in money is the
waste and loss of moral influence. "Ideally," it
has been said, "the Church is the social unifier;
practically, in many places, the churches, just
because there are several, are themselves the cause
of faction and discord." Whatever normal competition may be to the life of trade, we know what
"cut-throat" competition, that disregards the rules
of the game, may do for business. And however
good may be the purposes of the churches, the
competition, resulting when several are forced to
attempt to maintain their existence in a field only
large enough for one, is almost certain to provoke
jealousy and a narrowly sectarian and party spirit
that is fatal to Christian comity, as well as to alienate
from all the churches some of the finest elements in
the community. The spirit of rivalry repels the
indifferent observer and rubs the bloom from the
spirituality of those who indulge in it. Moral

leadership is incompatible with a schismatic spirit, and where the energies of the churches are consumed by the necessity of building up the institution for its own sake, there is no strength left for that free service of the community which is the price of influence. Thus the competition among the churches shuts them out in many a community from fields of social service where lie their largest opportunities.

The splitting up of the available religious forces in small communities, where they are weak at best, is suicidal. The report of the survey of Ohio, made in 1912 by the Board of Home Missions of the Presbyterian Church (North), reveals some significant facts which throw light upon the relation of size to efficiency. "The size of the membership of a church," it declares, "has a bearing upon its working efficiency too direct and important to permit us to neglect it here. There has been a great tendency in the country to multiply churches and denominations far beyond the number needed. This tendency is seen in the towns and villages, but its effects are not so clearly marked there. There are more churches in the country in proportion to the population than there are in the towns and villages, and especially are there more small and weak churches. . . . Of the 'town' churches only 8.7 per cent. have less than 25 members each, while 59.1 per cent. have over 100 members each. The 'town-country' churches average a little smaller; but 43.1 per cent. have over 100 members. Eighty-three per cent. of all country churches, however, have less than 100 members each, while 21.2 per cent. have each 25 members or less. Here we see in its clearest form the effects of strong denominational feeling upon church work. In the towns the multiplication of denominations, while often highly criminal from the point of view of church efficiency, is not so easily carried to an extreme. This, of course, is for the very obvious reason that there is a large number of people within an easy church-going radius upon whom these churches may draw. In the country the people are more scattered, and multiplication of churches and denominations means the dividing up of a clientele with very definite limits. Many churches were found which had a mere handful of members, sometimes but two or three, who were holding on to the old church long after some other church had come to fill the largest place in the religious life of the neighborhood, a policy which has very serious results. The impact of a small church upon society is necessarily slight. There is a momentum to large numbers. 'He that hath, to him shall be given.'

"We may indicate this by dividing the churches up into six groups according to the size of their membership, and giving the statistics of growth for each. These groups will be as follows: churches with a membership of 25 or less, 26 to 50, 51 to 100, 101 to 150, 151 to 200, and 201 and over.   In each of these groups there are included from 100 to 400 churches, enough to show clearly the tendencies.   The percentage of growing churches within each of these groups in the order given is as follows: 2.2 per cent., 16.6 per cent., 33.5 per cent., 48.2 per cent., 58.5 per cent., and 79 per cent.   The regularity with which the increase of efficiency and ability to survive parallels the increase in membership is very striking. Obviously, the great over-multiplication of small churches is one of the root causes of the failure of the country churches to meet the conditions which we have previously mentioned as affecting church efficiency.   They are unable to provide themselves with resident pastors who shall give them full service. They are unable to hold weekly public meetings. They are unable adequately to equip themselves for the work they must do.   The conclusion is unavoidable that the small church is a dying proposition. . . . Not until a church has at least 100 members does it have an even chance to survive."

Not all churches that are spared the disadvantages of the competition of rival organizations in small communities thrive spiritually, as has been said, or fully meet the needs of their constituency.   But where there is an average degree of consecration and intelligence in the membership and leadership, it is fair to say that they render a far more effective service than could be rendered if their strength were divided. In the recent study of two typical counties in New York and Vermont, already referred to, the authors say, "Among the smaller communities those with a single church are the only ones with a spirit of good cheer in church matters. The only township in Windsor county that has made a relative gain in church attendance and has also gained in benevolence and in total expenditures is a one-church township, while another one-church township (the only other in the county) stands second in these respects. . . . The figures for attendance, membership, and expenditures gathered in Tompkins county indicate how very various the evils of over-churching have become. Only four churches in the smaller communities in a twenty-year period have increased their activities in two or more of the three lines of activity considered above. Three of these are in one-church communities. The fourth is a weak church. Its expenditures were small in both periods, and its apparent gain in membership is due to padded rolls. Attendance figures furnish the best indication of the effect of over-churching. In small communities with only one church there was a loss of 29 per cent. in attendance in twenty

years. In small communities where there were two
churches there was a loss of 50 per cent., while in
the small communities of more than two churches
there was a loss of nearly 55 per cent."[1]

The cause of organized Christianity in communities where churches have been multiplied beyond the needs of the neighborhood and its ability
to sustain them will never prosper until such churches
combine in some form of co-operative union.   It is
imperatively necessary that the forces be united
if they are to win and hold the country districts
for Christ. Three forms of such combination have
been tested in various parts of the country until
they have passed the stage of experiment, two of
them applications of the federal principle, the third
a form of union still more complete. They are:
first, the church federation, such as has been already described, in which churches, worshiping
apart, unite for common tasks; second, the federated church, composed of two or more churches of
different denominations, each retaining its identity
and organization, but uniting for work and worship
under a single pastor; and third, the union denominational church, where two or more churches
of different denominations are merged to form a new
organization allied with the denomination of its
choice. The results of such experiments have

[1] Gill and Pinchot, *The Country Church*, pp. 144, 211.

at least demonstrated that, however serious may be the differences of opinion as to the most practicable forms in which Christian forces in over-churched rural communities may combine, combination in some form is the most hopeful means of meeting the conditions that confront them.

The church federation, the federated church, and the union church are related much as are friendship, partnership, and marriage; they stand for degrees of affiliation and identification of interest and activity. In communities where the problems arising from the multiplication of churches are not pressing, such a form of "church federation" as is described in the previous chapter is as effective in the country as in the city. Such organized co-operation is more than comity. Comity is negative in its implications: while it involves the cordial recognition on the part of one denomination of the Christian character of another, it is for the most part expressed in a policy of non-interference. Comity is inter-denominational courtesy: it is based upon mutual respect and esteem. It is fundamental, of course, to every form of co-operative effort, but it stops short of such co-operation. It involves regard for the rights of others, the avoidance of causes of offense and of encroachment upon another's field, respect for the rules of order and discipline that prevail in other communions,—in brief, all mutual consideration owed to one another by those who are engaged in a common cause. Where this is lacking, further co-operation is impossible.

While comity involves friendship, a church federation involves friendship cemented in a formal offensive and defensive alliance for the furthering of common ends. In such organized co-operation the churches concerned maintain their separate organizations, meetings for worship and ordinary activities, and unite only for such common tasks as cannot so well be done apart. Co-operative effort of this character ought to be more easily brought about and made effective in the smaller community than in the larger. Although it is not a form of combination adapted to the cure of the evils that spring from a plethora of churches, it will add dignity to the church in any community and immensely enhance its influence. When the churches thus speak and act together, voicing the conviction of the entire Christian fellowship and directing the full weight of its influence toward desirable ends, the whole community cannot but. heed. The natural field for such a co-operative federation, as has been said already, lies in those broad avenues of social service that lead to the purification of politics, the unification of charities, the protection of childhood and youth, the enforcement of law, the promotion of community studies, and the passing of good legislation. Churches of a like spirit and method may also profitably unite in evangelistic effort and stir and mold a whole population as a single church cannot hope to do. Such federation reveals the wealth of ideals in which all the churches share and draws the people of God together by the revelation of the degree of unity that exists below divisive differences, and prepares the ground for those more intimate forms of fellowship and co-operation which, in communities that are over-churched, make for economy and increased efficiency.

Another form of fellowship is known as "federated church," used here to describe those combinations of churches under the leadership of a single minister that are common in various parts of the country. From their prevalence in the Green Mountain State, this has been called "the Vermont plan." I do not speak here of the combinations of several churches of the same denomination under one itinerant minister, such as have always been common, but to the federation of two or more churches of different communions within the same section served by a single minister and worshiping in the same building. Where churches are separated more or less widely and are located in different communities, whether they are of the same or of different denominations, little is gained by their uniting in the support of a single minister except financial strength and the

superior quality of leadership that this usually
secures; and even this apparent benefit is generally
more than offset by the division of interest, and the
limited time that the minister can devote to each
constituent field. The influence of a church is sure
to suffer when the leader of its activities is not identified with the community to which it ministers.
He must have a stake in the community, must be
of it, if he is himself to be, or to lead his church to
be, a potent factor in its affairs.

No church can thrive under "absent treatment."
Merely to dip into the community at intervals, as
a comet into the solar system, and then retire to
some distant point inaccessible to his parishioners
until the period for return recurs, is not conducive to
the minister's usefulness, either in church or neighborhood. A district large enough to sustain a
church needs the entire time of the pastor of the
church. In the report of the rural survey of Ohio
made by the Presbyterian Board of Home Missions,
to which reference has already been made, it is said,
"There still remains in some sections an outworn
notion that it does not require a whole minister to
direct a country church; that the work of a country
church is easier than the work of a town or city
church. This notion is gradually being shocked out
of us, and we are discovering how hard it is to succeed and how easy it is to fail in the country field.

. . . A whole minister has a big enough task to keep a church alive, particularly in the country, as the records well show; a fraction of a minister has an infinitely more difficult task. The connection of the churches on a circuit is an important factor. Where the churches are so located that their respective parishes are practically contiguous, making one large parish with several preaching points, this system does not have such ill results. Where the churches are so located that their parishes are quite distinct and a considerable amount of travel is necessary to go from one to the other, the situation is more serious. In either event, however, the effect of this systematized vivisection upon church growth is unmistakable. Of all the churches with a whole minister each, 60 per cent. are growing. The few country churches that come in this class make as good a showing as the town churches. Six times out of ten the minister who can give his entire attention to one church succeeds in making it prosper. Probably this is as high a percentage of efficiency as any profession can show. Of the half-a-minister churches only 39 per cent. are growing. Of the third-of-a-minister churches only 35 per cent. are growing, while of those churches which have one-fourth of a minister or less, 26 per cent. are growing." Evidently one of the causes of the lack of strength in rural churches is the non-residence of the pastors, and the consequently fractional character of the service they are able to render. The absentee pastor is no more likely to cultivate successfully his spiritual vineyard than the absentee farmer is likely to produce good crops. "The success of the church and its continuance," declares the report of the survey dealing with conditions in Missouri, "are dependent upon the residence of the minister in the parish. The difficulties of the church and the danger of its extinction are greatly increased by a non-resident ministry." It may at least be said in favor of such a combination of churches of different denominations situated in a single community as we have now in mind, that it generally makes possible a resident ministry.

A one-minister plan has been tried in many places during the past twenty years with varying degrees of success. The details of method and organization differ widely according to conditions. It is an essential characteristic of the plan that the church organizations involved remain intact, each retaining its own denominational affiliations and contributing to its own objects of benevolence. Usually the pastors are chosen in succession from the ministry of the constituent denominations. Very often, and generally most widely, the union is entered into for a specified time only, and may be terminated at the expiration of the period at the desire of either party.

10

Success under this method, it need hardly be said, is impossible except upon the broadest basis of requirements for church membership. If it is to be truly a community church, all who love the Lord Jesus and who desire to labor for the coming of his kingdom must be welcomed. A successful church of this type at Freewater, Oregon, reports: "Among our members we now number Congregationalists, Presbyterians, Methodists, Christians, Baptists, German Lutherans, and Episcopalians." The widest liberty of conviction as to non-essentials, and of practice in the administration of the ordinances, particularly as to admission to the Lord's Table and as to the mode and subjects of baptism, must be permitted, and if the convictions of the minister in charge do not permit him to administer the ordinances as the individual member or candidate for membership desires, the services of a minister from a neighboring parish must be sought. Fortunately, such a spirit of tolerance and charity is increasing every day as "the thoughts of men are widened with the process of the suns."

The advantages of such a plan are evident. Many federated churches have secured a stronger and better paid ministry, resident upon the field, and a more adequate equipment; and this at a lower total expenditure. Where there is real union of spirit, such a federation is likely to take a place of moral leadership in the community impossible to any one church while the Christian forces are divided. The federated church in Freewater, Oregon, composed of a Congregational and a Presbyterian church, declares after two years' trial, "All are working together in harmony, making possible several things not attainable before. The Christian forces of the community now present a united front to the enemy, and instead of discord, proselyting, and small numbers, union and harmony prevail. . . . The church has attained the distinction of being called 'the town's church.' . . . It has called forth the respect and co-operation of many not otherwise connected with it. It is a community church, with the stamp of approval of the city officers and business men of the town. The membership has already crystallized into a strong working force for righteousness which will be far-reaching in its results."[1] Similar testimony comes from many quarters of the effectiveness of such a form of federation under favorable conditions and leadership.

An experiment of this sort, however, often encounters the gravest difficulties; and it is to be questioned whether there have not been more failures than successes in the trial of it. The *odium theologicum* dies hard, unfortunately, and the grace of God often

[1] From a leaflet of information issued by this church.

seems to be insufficiently appropriated to overcome the crotchets of his children! Sectarian principles, that have been so assiduously cultivated, and that are so deeply rooted, are not easily transplanted, even across the street, from one ecclesiastical garden-bed to another. Local rivalries with the irritations that they sometimes provoke are not easily forgotten, and since the churches that are the subjects of federation retain their respective identities, these are sometimes carried into the partnership and become disturbers of the peace. The minister in charge, who must necessarily retain ecclesiastical standing in a particular denominational body, often seems an alien to members of the denomination within the federated church to which he does not belong. "The fact is," writes an experienced leader in this form of church organization, "that when a Methodist is on the field, if the federation is between the Methodists and the Baptists, the Baptists pray for his removal, and when a Baptist pastor is on the field, the Methodists sit up all night praying for his removal, and by actual experience, after a five years' test, the united congregation is very little larger than either one of them was before the federation began." The question might be raised as to whether the churches under consideration have enough of the Christian spirit to make worth while the attempt to federate them.

The difficulties of administration, where the constituent bodies retain their individual organizations with separate sets of officers, are often extremely serious without discernible fault in any quarter. A broad-minded and efficient Christian worker in Vermont, where the idea originated, writes in answer to an inquiry, "Federation, where two or more churches get together for the support of one pastor, is an utter failure in Vermont and I believe will be everywhere."

Notable results in many experiments seem to promise permanent success for the federated church in certain localities. On the whole, however, this plan has not proved to be as successful as that of the complete union of churches into a single organization in affiliation with a particular denomination. This, the third of the methods of federation, may be distinguished as "the union denominational church."

Under such a title it is not meant to include those combinations of believers that exist in some localities in so-called union churches that sustain no denominational connection whatsoever, nor such as are composed of those holding elsewhere their ecclesiastical connections and uniting only for the purpose of common worship. Such organizations, unaffiliated with any general denominational body, are deprived of some of the essentials of strength and usefulness and tend to become mere preaching stations. They lack the stimulating fellowship of other churches, and are without incentive to missionary activity or channel for its expression in gifts of money or service. They tend to become isolated and self-centered and out of touch with the stream of religious interest and progress.

The union we are now considering is that of two or more churches of different denominations that unite to form a single church, either of one of the constituent denominations or of some other faith not represented in the combination. Thus a Baptist and a Methodist church in a community too small to support more than a single organization might unite, under this plan, to form either a Methodist or a Baptist church, or, if it should be deemed wise, they might choose to become a Congregational church. The essential features of such a plan of union are that the churches forming the combination shall not retain their original identity, nor their separate sets of officers, nor cut themselves loose from all denominational affiliations; but shall organize themselves into a new church that shall be a member of some one of the denominations already existing, thus retaining the stimulating influences of association with other bodies of Christians, and sharing the world-wide outlook of denominational activities and securing the benefits of the counsel and direction of the larger body to which they belong.

The possibility of unions of this nature might seem chimerical were it not for the fact that they have been accomplished in numerous localities and are growing more frequent. Such a plan avoids most of the difficulties which the federated churches are called upon to meet. It has, however, obstacles peculiar to itself with which to contend. The most obvious is the natural reluctance of any church to relinquish its identity. Even a failure does not always recognize failure, and never likes to admit it, particularly in the presence of an apparently successful rival. Which shall be the church to sacrifice its life upon the altar of efficiency? When that difficult question is decided, the problem of union is well on the way to solution. Blessed is that church, which, in the face of the crying needs of a community that only a united church can meet, has so caught the spirit of its Master as to believe that with the church, as with the disciple, to save life is to lose it, and that to lose life for Christ's sake and the gospel's is to find it!

It is essential, of course, to this form of union that the constituent churches shall deliberately put aside all divisive denominational peculiarities of polity and practice. Where conscientious convictions prevent this, the price is continued disunion.

If, for example, Congregationalists and Baptists are to unite to form a Baptist church, Congregationalists cannot impose sprinkling upon Baptists, nor Baptists immersion upon Congregationalists. So much is obvious. There is always the possibility of the establishment of a form of "associate membership" by which unimmersed believers may be affiliated with the church, but this is to take in members, as it were, by the back door, and is always an unsatisfactory makeshift. Either sprinkling must be frankly recognized as valid in essence and spirit if defective in form, or Baptists must cease to require baptism in any form as a prerequisite to church membership, and receive members on profession of faith alone, leaving the observance of the ordinance to the individual conscience, like their open-membership brethren in England. Similarly, if diverse elements are to unite in the organization of an Episcopal church, the Episcopalians must relinquish insistence upon the exclusive validity of ministerial orders episcopally derived on the basis of a doctrine of apostolic succession. Where such concessions are impossible, a union of churches is for the present impossible. These are but examples of practical difficulties that may arise, whatever denomination may be chosen by the union of forces. It is to avoid them that it is sometimes counted wise to organize the united church under a denomination other than that to which any of the churches concerned belongs. One thing only is essential: that the new church, whatever its affiliations, shall be flexible and tolerant, comprehensive and catholic, truly a community church.

This is the form of union, however brought about, that holds most promise for the future. When arranged through state denominational agencies, or by state interdenominational federations, so that the denominations involved shall each gain a union church where they consent to surrender a church to unite with one of another denomination, it promises best. As the federated church is known as "the Vermont plan," the credit for the promotion of the plan of reciprocal exchange of churches between denominations belongs to the Interdenominational Commission of Maine, the first of state church federations, which has long advocated it. The report of the Commission for 1914 declares, "Our Maine plan of reciprocal exchanges was recommended to the Federal Council of Churches of Christ in America in Chicago last December by the Home Missions Commission, and was approved by the Federal Council as the ideal for adoption in all parts of the country." The spirit and method of the plan are well described in another section of the report: For the purposes of preventive and constructive co-operation it was recommended:

1. That the denominations, through their supervising representatives, such as state agents, home missionaries, or presiding elders, report to the Commission the names of towns in which a union of churches may seem desirable, in order that the Commission may serve as a clearing-house and bureau of reciprocity.

2. That the Commission then shall consider the conditions in these several towns, the constituencies of the churches and the changes which would appear desirable for the best welfare of the community, and, when the Commission finds that an equitable exchange can be made so that in one town denomination A may surrender to denomination B its church interests, and in another town denomination B can surrender an equal interest to denomination A, then the Commission shall recommend to the two denominations such an exchange.

3. That such reciprocal exchanges shall be contemplated only between those denominations which distinctly commit themselves to the plan, and the interests of other denominations shall be in no wise molested by recommendations of the Commission.

4. It is recognized that this plan requires great care and consideration in its execution lest the prejudices and the feelings of local church-members be ignored and ideal states be sought which are not practical. Particularly must all conscientious scruples be carefully safeguarded and good feeling and brotherly love be preserved.

5. This plan distinctly confesses that the so-called "union" churches, while approved in some places, yet incur so many perils, through their lack of associational fellowship or superior ecclesiastical supervision, through having no larger missionary interests, home or foreign, and no approved ministry from which to secure pastoral care, as to be unwise organizations to encourage. This plan aims at consolidating religious

forces and leaving them within the limits of denominational fellowship.

The Rev. Josiah Strong, of the American Institute of Social Service, is quoted as saying, "The greatest need at the present time of this entire movement (toward the unification of Christian forces) is a practical vindication of the principles and methods of church union and federation in the smaller towns, villages, and hamlets." The pioneers in these experiments are rendering a service to the cause of the kingdom of God that can hardly be overestimated. Out of the present experimental stage are to come principles and methods that will guide the development of the future. Even the failures are instructive as showing ways to be avoided. It is something gained that we have come to see so clearly the necessities that compel some readjustment of religious forces in over-churched rural communities if the Church is to rise to its duties and opportunities. The future of the Church in America and the place that it is to hold in the developing life of the nation are dependent upon the progress of the spirit of Christian unity. "Organic church union at the top," *i. e.*, through the amalgamation of entire denominations, has thus far made slow progress; the immediate need is a larger number of successful examples of the possibility of "union at the bottom," in the co-operation and combination of individual churches of different denominations. The spirit of unity thus fostered at the base will make its way toward the summit. The greatest hindrances to-day are inertia, a narrow sectarianism, selfishness, and a lack of spiritual vision; but these are not inherent, and are not insurmountable. When the churches are more anxious to leaven the community with a saving gospel than to keep up denominational fences and to win a sectarian success, they will be willing to unite on essentials, whatever may become of non-essentials. The foggy thinking in which we lose ourselves and lose touch with our fellow-Christians will some day be dissipated when love floods in like the light and the mists and noxious vapors of the night fly before the ascending sun.

CO-OPERATION IN HOME MISSIONS

Combinations in business world.—Obstacles to co-operation in home mission effort.—Past methods of operation.—Conditions in the West demand the establishment of churches.—Problems presented by the complex nature of the population.—Successful operations of the American Sunday-School Union.—Home Missions Council.—Its organization, principles, and operations: investigations of particular sections of the country, reports of conditions as discovered.—Additional functions and powers suggested.

CHAPTER VII

CO-OPERATION IN HOME MISSIONS

WHEREVER we look, the competitive idea and spirit, both in theory and in practice, is giving way before the modern principle of co-operation. In social theory and experiment, the thought of our day moves from individualism toward collectivism. In politics, party lines are breaking down and men of diverse theories are uniting for the attainment of practical ends. In the industrial, and commercial, and financial worlds, combination spells success. "Efficiency" is the new word on everybody's lips, and to the stern test of its requirements all the processes of the business world must be brought. Not less must the methods of every religious enterprise be judged in terms of efficiency, for the evangelization of the world pre-eminently deserves the name of "big business." Waste of time and effort, reduplication, unnecessary expense of any kind are less defensible here than elsewhere. The real difficulty in this field, however, arises from the attempt of conscientious men to discriminate between waste and necessary expenditure, and to discover how far it is possible for Christian people, with their differences

159

of religious views, to combine their forces for economy of effort.

There are peculiar obstacles in the way of full co-operation between the churches in home missionary effort. On the frontier, denominations contest for new territory. Their prosperity and growth depend upon pushing forward and occupying the points that promise some day to be strategic. All the motives of denominational pride and ambition, together with a sincere fidelity to denominational convictions and downright earnestness of religious purpose, combine to urge the churches to occupy the new districts at the earliest possible moment. The necessity for comity and co-operation in home missionary enterprises arises from the fact that these impulses, working in all denominations alike, drive them in the same directions, and tempt all to occupy those localities that give most promise of becoming centers of influence. "As soon as a town was opened," said a speaker at the Chicago meeting of the Federal Council, "the denominations used to hurry into it: Episcopalians in the parlor-car, Presbyterians in the sleeper, Congregationalists in the day coach, Baptists on the tender, and Methodists on the cow-catcher; and by the time those in the passenger coaches had unlimbered, the Baptists and the Methodists were building their chapels. Very soon the problem was how to get some of the denominations out!" For years the various sects have labored at the task of winning the new empire of America for Christ, each with its independent plan of campaign as though it alone were in the field, without consultation or co-operation, or troubling to acquaint itself with the methods or results of the activities of others engaged in the same enterprise.

Reassuring signs of a better day are appearing. The task is so great—nothing less than the conquest and development of a new nation—and the need so appalling, and the results of such guerrilla warfare so meager in comparison with the need, that the denominations have been driven to join hand, and heart, and will, in their common work of evangelization. Here are almost 100,000,000 of the most energetic and progressive people under the sun, in a territory vast and rich enough to support a population twenty times its size, pressing forward in an irresistible tide into the sparsely settled regions on the western slope of the continent; eager for gain, ready for privation and sacrifice in the pursuit of it, needing the touch of that idealism that alone can redeem such ambition from sordid greed, and presenting an unexampled opportunity for the ministration of the Church which alone can furnish the altruistic impulse. On the broad prairies, towns spring up almost over night, and the plowshare of the pioneer turning over the unbroken sod transforms

11

the rolling plains into waving fields of grain. Vast
irrigation projects convert waste places into a luxu-
riant garden and cause the desert to blossom as the
rose. Everywhere upon the frontier, homes are
hardly built before schools are planted among them;
but the saloon and gambling house are quick to follow in the wake of progress. If such new territories
are to be won for God and righteousness, the church
must be early upon the field and make its contribution to their development during the early, formative
years.

It is the prosperity of America that is, in part, its
peril. The story is told of a soldier in the army of
Antigonus who became conspicuous for his bravery
upon the field of battle. With invincible courage
he faced the most overwhelming odds, led forlorn
hopes to victory, was foremost in the charge and last
in retreat. Attracting the attention and admiration
of his officers, he was brought into the presence of the
general. On inquiry it was found that the man was
poor and afflicted with a distressing and painful disease. In pity the general bestowed money upon
him, and placed him under the care of his best physicians, who soon relieved him of his malady. But it
was quickly discovered that the soldier had lost his
enterprise and courage. He no longer led the
charge. Formerly the very discomfort and suffering which distressed him had driven him forth to

every desperate endeavor; now he sought his ease, for, as he remarked to his comrades, he had something worth living for—health, home, family, and other comforts, and life under these conditions was too valuable to risk. Such is the peril of prosperity, —an ignoble content, a cowardly conservatism, a base materialism, a self-centered satisfaction with things as they are, a blind indifference to the compulsion of great causes, a regard for the body of things and a contempt for their soul. Above all, because of its prosperity and promise of material good, America needs the offices of religion.

Toward this land of plenty, as to another Canaan, the peoples of the older world, oppressed by poverty, are flowing in a steady stream of a million or more a year. As an ever-increasing proportion of this immigration comes from the south and east of Europe, the problems which it offers grow more acute and grave. What are we to do with these eager folk who press upon us, ignorant, most of them, of our language and of our institutions, with contrary social and political traditions and ideals, and of another spiritual heritage? What, rather, are they to do with us? Are these unassimilated masses to despoil our institutions and remove our landmarks, and to make of the descendants of the Puritans strangers in an alien land? And what shall we say of the 10,000,000 negroes whose ancestors immigrated against their will, and who now share our inheritance?   No scheme of colonization will solve this problem: they are here to stay. The day is not very far distant when these 10,000,000 will have become 20,000,000. We cannot hope that the masses of the negro population can remain in ignorance, living in squalor and poverty, without the contamination of such conditions spreading throughout the commonwealths in which they reside. We cannot have ignorance, or poverty, or vice anywhere in the community without its affecting the entire population.   Add to these elements that go to make up the urgent problem of American life, the pitiful necessities of the Indian wards of the nation; the menace of Mormonism; and the growing numbers of those who come to us from Mohammedan lands, from the minarets of whose more than threescore temples on this continent there daily sounds the muezzin's call to prayer; and we may see how large looms the task committed to the evangelical churches of America.

Similar and related to this problem of a complex population is the engrossing and insistent problem of the American city, to which the larger proportion of our immigration flows. To-day the city dominates our civilization,—socially, politically, and religiously. Whereas in 1800 one in twenty of the population dwelt in the city, in 1900 the proportion was one in three; and with the development of our manufactures it will not be long before one-half of the people will assuredly be found residing in municipalities. Already one-half of the population of the Empire State lives in New York City. Not Springfield, but Chicago, is the political, and social, and commercial capital of Illinois. America gets its ideals from the city: as goes the city, so goes the nation. If there is corruption in the city, the whole body politic suffers. If the saloon rules the city, the country will not escape. If the government of our cities is the scandal of American life, then republican institutions the nation over are imperiled. If there is contempt for law there, the power of the law languishes elsewhere. The political problem is largely a city problem. A Christian civilization is on trial in the city. And if the city church fails, we cannot hope to redeem that failure by conquests in the town and countryside.

Such conditions are a challenge to the faith and consecration of the Christian Church; and it is becoming increasingly evident that no single communion is sufficient to meet them. To these vast, unassimilated masses in the very center of our population, who come to us from other lands, there must be brought the finest products of a Christian civilization. If these are to be Americanized, a large share in the task will devolve upon the Church. With a magnificent optimism, Senator Hoar of Massachusetts, shortly before his death, declared, "I believe that if all Americans of native birth should die to-morrow, the masses who have come to us from other shores may be trusted to preserve and carry to success the spirit of American institutions;" but such hopefulness would be only complacent folly unless adequate efforts are made to imbue these millions with that spirit in its best estate. The negro must be evangelized and taught, the Indian protected from his weaknesses and his enemies, Mormonism checked and its venom extracted, and the frontier communities molded and inspired by the influences of religion. The island possessions of the new America, moreover, must be evangelized. Competition in these high tasks is folly; the competitive spirit defeats its own ends. Only co-operation can win America for Christ.

The pioneer among agencies which have applied themselves to the solution of these problems is the American Sunday-School Union, whose fruitful service has extended over the last 98 years. Believing that through an interdenominational rather than a denominational effort the Christian Church can most effectively reach the isolated and neglected rural districts all over the United States, it has sent its missionaries into the remotest corners of the land, rallying the Christian forces, however small or crude, and planting union Sunday-schools to serve as the

nuclei of Christian activity. The annual report of
the Union for 1915 describes the labors of ten district superintendents, under whom are 224 general
or local missionaries serving fields each covering from
one to a dozen counties. These missionaries are
constantly engaged in studying religious conditions in their fields, especially in rural and isolated
districts. Where such communities are without
Sunday-schools, interest is aroused by house-to-
house visitation, teachers and officers are enlisted,
and Sunday-schools organized. During the year
covered by this report, these field workers organized
1,368 new schools and reorganized 687. Many an
abandoned church has been rehabilitated through
the organization within it of such a union Sunday-
school. "Not infrequently," declares the report
for 1914, "in communities where two denominational
churches have been closed for years, the missionary,
by determining 'not to know anything among you
save Jesus Christ and him crucified,' brings the
people, who in the past had been in different denominations, into one united congregation, identified with a denomination of their own choosing."
Seventy-eight congregations were organized last
year and transferred from the care of the American
Sunday-School Union to denominational control.
The pioneer work could have been only non-
denominational in the true sense, since these 78

churches were divided among 14 different denominations.

The organization through which the Home Mission Boards of the Protestant churches of America are seeking to correlate their missionary forces is the Home Missions Council. Organized as recently as 1908, it is now composed of representatives of 33 societies and boards connected with 21 distinct denominations, embodying nine-tenths of the nationally organized home mission forces. This organization holds regular meetings twice a year for the consideration of great administrative questions, and through its special committees and deputations seeks to determine the facts that compose the home mission problem, and to further co-operative effort. The spirit in which it pursues its task is evident in the principles which, in conjunction with the Commission on Home Missions of the Federal Council of Churches of Christ in America, it has lately formulated and recommended to the Home Mission Boards of the denominations co-operating. It instructs its representatives:

1. To confer with like officers of other Home Mission Societies or Boards and arrange to allot the entirely unoccupied fields among the various bodies so that each shall feel a special responsibility for given fields.

2. To decline application for Home Mission aid at any place where the gospel of Christ is earnestly and adequately

promulgated by others and where assured prospects of growth do not seem to demand the establishment of other churches.

At least ten of the national Home Mission Societies and Boards, including all but one of the large denominations, have given their explicit endorsement to these principles. While the spirit of the administrative officers of all the leading boards is in full harmony with such a program, it cannot be denied that there are multitudes of people, ministers, missionaries, and laymen, in every communion, who have not yet reached an equal height and breadth of view. It is the membership at large which determines the actual policy to be pursued even within denominations that are least democratic in polity. That this is still, in many quarters, directed along the old competitive lines, is not so much the fault of the leaders as of the local administrators at the front.

The organization of the Home Missions Council has made possible a co-operative study of the various elements that compose the home mission problem. During 1914, for example, the Council's Committee on Immigrant Work conducted an extensive inquiry concerning the immigrant population of the United States, including in its surveys the Bohemians, Poles, and Magyars, and, less completely, the Finns, Croatians, Serbs, Armenians, and other nationalities. The results of these studies not only revealed the meagerness of the total work carried on by the allied denominations, but, in the words of the committee, "made renewedly clear the irrelevancy of our denominational distinctions in this field, save as in a few cases the people ministered to come from nations having a considerable Protestant tradition."

For the first time in the history of the home mission enterprise, it has become possible, also, through the Council, to make careful and comprehensive investigations of particular sections of the country to determine the conditions actually existing and the genuine needs of the fields. These studies or surveys, made during 1913 and 1914, were initiated by a deputation of board secretaries in a series of "consultations" with members of state boards and committees, state and district superintendents, and other field administrators of home mission work in 15 of the western states. After the preliminary consultation, each conference selected a state survey committee composed of representatives of each religious body co-operating, who have been publishing the results of their investigations in a series of bulletins. The first deals with a general survey of the entire territory under observation, including those states in which the largest proportion of the funds contributed to the treasuries of home mission boards and national societies are applied in various forms of evangelization and church extension. Later bulletins are devoted to the results of more intensive surveys of Oregon, North Dakota, Colorado, Northern California, and Washington. While the region examined embraces almost one-half of our continental territory, only 13.7 per cent. of the total population is now found within it; and while the average density of population for the country at large is 30.9 per square mile, that for this region is only 8.8. During the past decade this vast territory has increased its population at a rate double that of the increase of the country as a whole, and evidently will soon include a population commensurate with its size. Thus is suggested something of the "civilization-building, and the consequent strain upon social institutions, which this region will experience in the next few decades." Not one of the states under observation shows a percentage of Protestant church membership to population equal to that for the country taken as a whole, while six of the states show Roman Catholic percentages exceeding that for the entire country.

Considerable attention has been given in an earlier chapter to the "overlapping" of religious agencies. This is a serious condition, occasioning waste of money, time, and energy. It is also the cause of much hostile criticism of the Church and its

methods. But reports of its prevalence may easily
be exaggerated and, as a matter of fact, the surveys
of the Home Missions Council indicate that on the
frontier, at least, it is a negligible factor in its effect
upon the efficiency of American Christianity com-
pared with that of "overlooking," or the neglect
by all denominational forces of large sections of the
population. In an investigation of the state of
Colorado, made within a few years by the Commission on Home Missions of the Federal Council,
while many instances of an unwise reduplication of
church organizations were discovered,—such as that
of a town of 400 people with four churches, all sup-
ported by home mission aid,—133 communities were
reported, ranging from 150 to 1,000 souls, without
Protestant churches of any name, 100 of them being
also without a Roman Catholic church.

The study of 15 states undertaken by the Home
Missions Council was appropriately called "The
Neglected Fields Survey." Of one of the states it
is reported that it may be conservatively estimated
that at least 458 school districts have groups of
people living more than four miles from the nearest
church, and that these groups comprise at least
32,796 persons. From a township in this state with
a population of 300 the report was received, "There
is not a church of any kind in the township, nor any
religious services of any kind. There are only about

20 Catholics and 20 Lutherans who profess any religion." Such conditions are common in most of the
states surveyed. Of the districts in Oregon reporting, 54.1 per cent. have no church or Sunday-school
activities, and it is estimated that 33,000 school
children in the state reside in districts not supplied
with organized religious work. "I have lived here
11 years," writes one correspondent, "and I think
there have not been more than seven sermons
preached in this district in that time." Others
report not having had services in 15 or 20 years.
"It is safe to say," states the report for Colorado,
"making allowances for the fact that returns were
received from only 55 per cent. of the districts in the
state, that at least 25,000 or 30,000 people in
Colorado live more than four miles by a practicable
route of travel from the nearest church. Naturally
many of these people live in small communities scattered over a large area, making church work, as it
is usually done, impracticable. However, that is
not true of all, as is indicated by the fact that one
district with a population of 716 reports 'seven or
eight saloons, no church, one service per month;'
and another, with a population of 460, reports that
'the saloon is doing all that is being done.'"
"Throughout Washington and Oregon," writes
Dr. Ward Platt, of conditions prevailing seven years
ago, "may be found scores of narrow valleys teem-

ing with people.   No one is doing anything for them religiously, as but little is attempted by any church for Washington or Oregon outside the towns.   In southwestern Oregon is a county of about 1,500 square miles in which live at least 2,500 people, mostly American; and no denomination, according to the report made last year, is doing any work whatever in that whole county.   They are absolutely without church privileges."[1]   One in charge of a large field in western Washington declares, that "in his division only 209 towns out of 1,146 have church organizations, leaving 937 towns and villages without any religious privileges whatever. Over half the children in western Washington have never been enrolled in a Sunday-school.   The whole region is in its infancy and is developing with astounding rapidity."   "Where in this race," asks Dr. Platt, "is the Church of God?"

It ought to be said, however, that since these statements were made by Dr. Platt, conditions in this section of the country have, without doubt, much improved as the field has been more fully occupied by evangelizing agencies.   During the four years closing in 1914, the American Sunday-School Union alone has increased the number of its missionaries in Washington, Oregon, and Idaho to 11. Through their efforts 400 new Sunday-schools were

[1] Ward Platt, *The Frontier*, p. 106.

organized, with 1,400 teachers and almost 12,000 pupils; prayer-meetings and young people's societies were established in large numbers, and over 1,000 persons professed conversion. Out of the Sunday-schools thus established, 14 churches of different denominations were organized. That deplorable need of further efforts still exists, however, in many districts of the far West is indicated in the following summary in the report of the Neglected Fields Survey Committee to the Home Missions Council at its meeting in 1914: "In Oregon 30.7 per cent. of the districts sending in returns have churches and Sunday-schools; in North Dakota, 27.7 per cent.; in Colorado, 26.6 per cent.; in California (northern portion), 28 per cent.; in Washington, 32.7 per cent. While many districts reporting failed to reply to the question as to whether there was immediate religious activity, the percentages of those definitely reporting no religious activity are: in Washington, 40.1 per cent.; in California (northern portion), 36.9 per cent.; in Colorado, 25.4 per cent."

The final report of the committee which directed these surveys, made to the Council at its meeting in 1915, declared that, "in the 6,515 school districts reported upon, the best state had 44 per cent. without any kind of a church or Sunday-school, and the worst 64 per cent.; and that each state showed from 25,000 to 47,000 people living more than four miles from any church." "Perhaps more significant," the report continues, "is the fact that even where churches of some kind are reported, it is shown that they are not pouring through the community a continuous stream of life. Thirty-five per cent. of them hold less than four services a month. But even of those which have more or less preaching, a large proportion are without continuous ministry. From 31 to 51 per cent. have no resident pastors."

It was to study and to meet such conditions by concerted action that the Home Missions Council was organized. It is not the intention of the Council to foster the organization of union or interdenominational churches, since, as it believes, the history of such organizations, deprived of denominational influence and control, is not encouraging. Wherever churches should be combined, the Council recommends that it be done by the method of reciprocal exchange between denominations, according to the method described in the preceding chapter; with provision for receiving into associate or full membership in such denominational organizations the members of any other communion as shall make them truly community churches. Yet the Council does not take upon itself the function of interfering in the disposition of the affairs of individual churches: it can do no more than make recommendations, leaving local adjustments to be administered by those upon the field. It is not the purpose of the Council to decrease or hinder the work of any denomination, but rather to stimulate the activities of every Christian body, and to encourage particular denominations to enter specified fields that are unoccupied or neglected. It advocates no theoretical scheme of Christian unity, but stands for the most practical forms of co-operative effort that are immediately possible. It seeks, moreover, to systematize and correlate those forms of work in which the denominations are already engaged in common, as, for example, educational work for the Indians, and, where possible, to employ a single agency for tasks better accomplished by union effort, as is instanced in the appointment by the Council of a traveling evangelist among the Hindus in America.

In the effort to devise a plan for co-operative action, in view of the facts revealed by the "Survey of Neglected Fields," a series of conferences was held by the committee in six western states during 1914, with results the importance of which for the future of the home mission enterprise can hardly be overestimated. A federation for the more effective conduct of home missions was instituted in every state, or existing federations further developed. The plan projected in Utah, which has already

12

been adopted by all of the state and national boards and ecclesiastical bodies affected by it that have thus far taken definite action upon it, and upon whose favorable consideration its initiation depends, is of the utmost significance as indicating the trend of the new co-operative principle of our home mission agencies. In outline,[1] the plan calls for the organization of a Utah Interdenominational Commission, to be composed of two persons appointed by the state organization officially representing each religious body co-operating, a secretary of each supporting national board having *ex officio* membership. To this Commission general policies of co-operative work within the state are to be submitted for advisement, and by it sums to be used in the co-operative work are to be determined, and such other duties discharged as shall be jointly assigned by the co-operating religious bodies. In addition, a Utah Home Mission Workers' Council is contemplated, to be composed of four workers chosen by each religious body co-operating, this Council "to promote co-operative work in the field, advise in the adjustment of differences, arrange for the effective use of funds assigned to the co-operative budget, and increase by all practicable means the efficiency of the work of all the co-operating agencies throughout the state." It is proposed to

[1] Report of Home Missions Council for 1915, p. 129.

organize also an Annual Utah Workers' Institute of
three or more days' duration, to be of an educational
character, designed to inspire and train workers for
efficient service, open to every ordained minister,
mission-school teacher, or other worker in the state,
with the necessary expense of attendance to be paid
in every case by such methods as each denomination
may adopt. It is provided in the plan that "action
of the Council affecting established home mission
policies, enlargement of co-operative budgets, or the
relations of denominations, shall be undertaken only
after the concurrence of the Commission." Finally,
it is agreed that the plan "does not contemplate the
curtailing of denominational autonomy, nor encroach
upon the prerogative of the ecclesiastical bodies co-
operating, except as herein provided, or as each and
all may later agree."

This plan, if successfully instituted, appears to be
adapted to bring the dream of a co-operative Christendom down from heaven to earth. Foreign Mission agencies, as we shall see in the following chapter, possess the instrument through which their
efforts may be correlated and unified. The Home
Missions Council suffices to bring together the
leaders in home mission endeavor, and makes possible the formulation of broadly inclusive plans.
The great deficiency has been the lack of a plan by
which the co-operative spirit could be conveyed to

the point of actual application to specific religious tasks. The actual responsibility for the expensive and wasteful competitive methods prevalent particularly in rural communities rests, for the most part, upon state denominational organizations, and these, in most instances, are carrying on their work without systematic co-operation in the occupation of fields, or even conference with one another. In a few states, as in Maine, state federations of churches concern themselves with particular problems of comity and co-operation, but such federations, in general, are so loosely organized that they are in constant danger of degenerating into select *coteries* for the ineffective if innocuous discussion of doctrinal agreements and differences. There is imperative need either that larger discretionary and executive powers shall be delegated to such federations for the settlement of particular questions of comity and co-operation as they arise, or that, by some such plan as that of Utah, those responsible for the direction of denominational efforts within the state shall regularly meet for the discussion and mutual adjustment of the projects and methods of their denominations, and for the correlation of the forces which they control.

Thus the Home Missions Council is breaking out new paths in the field of interdenominational co-operation. It is making it possible for the denominations included within it thoroughly to study the facts that enter into the home mission problem as no single denomination is able to study them, and then to plan a united campaign to disseminate knowledge of the facts and to meet the needs that are disclosed. It involves no slackening of the bonds of denominational loyalty or loss in the force of denominational conviction. But it is based on the assumption that the character of the differences that separate the affiliated denominations is not such as to prevent co-operation in the tremendous task of the evangelization of the continent, and that it is not essential to the spiritual welfare of America that the entire population should become Methodist or Presbyterian, or members of any particular denomination, so long as all are Christian, and the springs of national and personal life are purified and sweetened. It is a long step forward that the churches are definitely agreed that God does not plan to save America by means of any one denomination, and that a broader avenue has been discovered along which the forces of Protestant Christianity may march together.

CO-OPERATION ON THE FOREIGN
MISSION FIELD

Extent and difficulties of the foreign missionary effort.—
Heathen themselves impressed with conflicting Christian
teachings.—Oriental Christians not interested in causes and
conditions that gave birth to the various denominations.—
A new spirit of co-operation: its nature and possibilities.—
Development of Christian unity on mission fields as indicated
in reports of Continuation Committee Conferences in India,
China, Korea, and Japan.—Attitude of the churches in the
East toward denominational supervision.—Work of co-op-
eration in the fields of Christian education and medicine.—
Co-operation between foreign missionary organizations in
America.—Unity among churches of the East greatest in-
fluence for co-operation at home.

CHAPTER VIII

CO-OPERATION ON THE FOREIGN MISSION FIELD

It is against the dark background of the needs of heathenism that the real significance and the cost of the divided state of Christendom are most clearly revealed. The churches of Christ are definitely committed to the task of evangelizing 1,000,000,000 souls, massed in great centers of population, or widely scattered over vast tracts of territory, and spread over every zone from the icy coasts of the Esquimos to the tropic jungles of Africa and the frozen islands of the southernmost seas. The gospel of Christ must be interpreted into each language and racial temperament until every man upon the earth may hear the truth in the tongue to which he was born. The missionary must penetrate into tropical regions where existence is almost impossible for men reared in the temperate zone, prejudices must be removed, institutions must be organized, a new spiritual atmosphere must be created, and the great streams of racial development must be turned into new channels.

It is a titanic enterprise, the most stupendous undertaking that has ever appealed to the soul of

man. Obviously it will tax the resources of the
entire Church to the utmost.   If all Christians everywhere should join in cordial co-operation, marching
together as one great army in a single campaign, so
distributing their forces as to economize time, and
effort, and money, minimize prejudice and opposition, and utilize, to the highest degree of efficiency,
all the armament of Christendom, marshaling the
combined resources of the Church with a superlative
strategy, and meeting the solid front of heathenism
with a united and unshaken vigor of attack, the
most hopeful might even then despair at times and
the stoutest hearts lose courage. Yet, among the
obstacles that oppose the progress of the gospel of
Christ among heathen peoples, one of the greatest
is the lack of union among the forces that are engaged in the propaganda.

Not only must the missionaries meet the natural
and inevitable prejudice that confronts a new and
strange philosophy, and all the inertia of spiritual
lethargy, but they must labor against the misunder-
standings and confusion that they are themselves
forced to introduce through the presentation of
various and conflicting types of the religion which
they seek to inculcate.   It is not uncommon to-day
for missionaries to be bidden by heathen folk first
to reconcile their own differences before seeking to
win converts to their faith,—a situation sure to be

more often met as, with the wider spread of Christianity, heathen opposition grows stronger and more intelligent. "Which is the bigger God," asked a chief in Africa, "the Presbyterian God, or the Baptist God, or the Methodist God?" "What is the answer," asks a friend of the missionary enterprise, "to the Japanese nobleman crossing the public square of Tokio, who, urged to become a Christian, sweeps his hand about the square where a score or more missionary agencies have their homes, and asks, 'Which Christianity?'" Is it any wonder that the heathen peoples stand dismayed upon the threshold of the temple of the new religion that claims the right to displace their ancestral faiths, at the multiplicity of varieties and the differences and divisions among those who already worship at its altars, and the diverse and often discordant voices that appeal from its pulpits? To which of these is their allegiance to be given, and whom must they believe? "The world will never be converted by a disunited church."[1] At a conference of Christian workers recently held in China, a Chinese leader said, "In our town are four different translations of the Bible, and they cause great trouble by reason of their differences." A physician rose and remarked, "I have just come from the sick-bed of a man who had had eleven native physicians who had

---

[1] William Milligan, *The Resurrection of Our Lord*, p. 202.

each left a different prescription. The patient had not taken any one of them. I am for Christian unity."

It is inevitable that the causes responsible for the division of the Church into various bodies in Christian lands should fail to impress the minds of those of other races of so different a spiritual heritage and history. It is impossible that these should enter sympathetically into the struggles and sacrifices and toils which have been the price of spiritual freedom. They discern only the differences that have resulted, devoid of the glow and warmth borrowed from the circumstances of their origin and history, and the contemplation of them leaves the converts from heathenism unmoved and cold. No enthusiasm of loyalty unites the heart of the Chinaman to a denominational banner inscribed with the name of a geographical division of a territory remote from his own, and which has no meaning whatsoever when transported across the sea. It excites no pride in his heart to be a member of the Methodist Episcopal Church South, especially if the Chinese members of the Methodist Episcopal Church North are situated to the south of him. Bishop Thoburn has expressed the amusement, mingled with sadness, with which he heard an almost naked Hindu Christian assert that he was a "Scotch Presbyterian!"

The rising spirit of nationalism in every Asiatic land finds no satisfaction in such artificial distinctions imported from abroad. It is as unjust as it is unwise to seek to impose upon these Eastern peoples distinctions and divisions which, however much they may mean to those among whom they originated, can never mean anything to them but the shibboleths of a strife in which they have had no share and can have no interest. The churches beyond the seas have not been won by the proclamation of our points of difference, but by the gospel that we hold in common. The native Christians of China who laid down their lives by the thousand in the dreadful days of the Boxer riots would not have died for a form of baptism, nor for a scheme of church polity, nor for a liturgy, nor for a theory of the validity of ecclesiastical orders; but they refused to trample upon the figure of a rude cross traced on the ground, though their lives were required as the alternative offered in exchange, lest they dishonor the Lord of Christendom! For the Christ of the Cross multitudes even dared to die! It is always the Saviour that attracts and unites, and human interpretations and obscurations of him that repel and divide. The only bond that holds the Oriental to the particular denomination in which he is enrolled is the fact that this denomination, rather than another, brought him to Christ.

As a matter of fact, the names of many of the denominations do not find corresponding terms in the languages of some of the lands to which they are carried into which they can be translated, and have to be taken over bodily by transliteration, and the distinctions which they convey are in many cases so foreign to the habits of thought of such peoples that they never grasp their true significance. The real evils from which the nations suffer are impurity, social inequality, and despair. The African and the Korean feel their need of the Christ as soon as they understand him, for only Christ can reveal the character of God and thus rebuke impurity; only Christ can teach the brotherhood of man and so redeem the outcast; and only Christ can lift the veil from the future and exchange hope for hopelessness. But they do not feel the need, nor discern the force of the fine distinctions of doctrines for which denominationalism stands. Why should the conscience of the new-born convert be burdened with a mass of *Aberglaube* which can neither save nor condemn?

Further, if it were not for the pressure exerted from the home lands, the native Christians among these far-away peoples would speedily unite. "We should have one united Chinese Church in China," said a native leader there, "but the Mandarins in America will not permit it." Dr. A. J. Brown refers to "the grim remark of an East Indian pastor that, 'were it not for the vigilance of the Western shepherds, the Indian sheep would some fine morning be all found in one fold.'" A Chinese clergyman, the same author reports, in a union meeting of the churches about Nanking, arose and said, as he pointed in turn to several missionaries, "You are an American Presbyterian; and you can't help it, for you were brought up that way. You are a Canadian Methodist; and you can't help it, for you were brought up that way. You are an English Churchman; and you can't help it either, for you were brought up that way. But we are Chinese Christians, and we do not propose to permit you men from abroad to keep us apart." The new nationalism which is working like yeast in China and India to unify and energize these peoples, and which has already done its work in Japan, is impatient with a foreign church imposed upon it from without. Where native churches have been well established, the missionaries soon find that they must learn to be content to be simply the advisers and guides of a Christian community determined to develop along lines characteristic of its own civilization, and in forms indigenous to it. And that such is the case every true missionary rejoices, for the hope of heathenism lies in the development of a truly native church, with an energy and an enthusiasm derived immediately from the one Lord of the Church. The anxiety of the missionary is only lest the churches of Asia should demand their freedom before they have developed a native leadership fitted to guide it.

"If we want to win the heathen world to Christ," said Phillips Brooks, after his missionary tour around the world, "we must not go to them as Episcopalians, Presbyterians, Methodists, or Baptists: we must go to them simply as Christians." Dr. John R. Mott said to the great Edinburgh Missionary Conference that the union of the Church would mean more than the doubling of the missionary force. The difficulties in the way of the unification of the forces upon missionary fields are great; but if the foregoing statement is true, every possible effort should be made to surmount them.

The denominations which have been instrumental in founding mission churches are not to blame for the introduction of their distinctive and divisive principles into missionary lands. Such was the inevitable consequence of the denominational system. Any other course would have been impossible a century ago. The noble ideal of the London Missionary Society, founded in 1795, and composed of Presbyterians, Independents, and members of the Church of England, failed because it was too far in advance of its times. It declared its design to be "not to send Presbyterianism, Episcopalianism, or any form of church government (about which there may be differences of opinion among serious persons), but the glorious gospel of the blessed God to the heathen, and that it shall be left (as it ought to be left) to the minds of the persons whom God may call to the fellowship of his Son from among them, to assume for themselves such form of church government as to them shall appear most agreeable to the word of God." Later, however, as the missionary enterprise grew in extent, the Episcopalians and the Presbyterians withdrew to form missionary organizations of their own. Nevertheless this broad conception may prove to have been prophetic of the missionary method yet to be, though in that age it was impossible.

When we survey the missionary field to-day, it is evident that a new spirit of co-operation is flowing in everywhere like a flood. And something of what the character of that co-operation is to be when it is consummated is also becoming evident. It cannot come through compromise: it must come through comprehension. The distinctive convictions for which the various denominations stand cannot be cast aside like an outworn cloak without strain to conscience and consequent loss of spiritual power. But together with fidelity to distinctive principles there may and must be a new emphasis upon the things held in common as the essential

13

and permanent message of the Church. It is not essential that churches should be organized upon the basis of their peculiarities. It is possible to create a more inclusive fellowship to which each company of believers shall bring its particular interpretation of the Christ and add it to the common store. "In essentials unity, in non-essentials liberty, and in all things charity" is the motto for a united Church at home and abroad. Toward such an ideal the forces upon the foreign field, impelled by an appalling need and by the genius of the peoples among whom they labor, are earnestly striving. A missionary leader, recently returned from a tour in China and Japan, reports that he met in conference five Christian professors in the Doshisha University who united in the expression of belief that, while the essence of Christianity is bound to prevail in Japan, Western ecclesiastical forms and institutions will not prevail there.

Meanwhile, as we wait for the realization of an ideal unity, there must be a larger measure of cooperation in the survey of unoccupied fields, a more strict division of territory among the missionary agencies, a freer exchange of members between all types of churches, and a closer affiliation of all forms of service where co-operation or union is already possible. In mission lands, as at home, federation will precede organic unity. There is not a Baptist and a Presbyterian *materia medica*, nor has any single denomination a monopoly of the multiplication table.   Hospitals and medical schools are coming together everywhere, and in primary and secondary schools, wherever these can be administered more economically by uniting with other schools of a similar character of another denomination, consolidation is being promoted.   In the higher schools and colleges, and even in theological seminaries, the same tendency is evident.   The work of publication, in many centers, is accomplished for several denominations through a single agency.   Thus is the way being cleared for the closer spiritual unity that shall clearly fulfil the prayer of our Lord.

The reports of the Continuation Committee Conferences in Asia, held in India, China, Korea, and Japan, under the direction of Dr. John R. Mott during 1912–1913, indicate the notable progress of recent years both in the growth of the spirit of Christian unity and in its practical exemplification upon the missionary field.   In the official reports of each of the local conferences held at Madras, Bombay, Jubbulpore, Allahabad, and Calcutta, reference is made to the wide-spread desire on the part of the native Christians of India, especially among the better educated, "for the development of one united Indian Church."   At the India National Conference in Calcutta the following minute was adopted:

"This Conference is of the opinion that there is undoubtedly a strong desire on the part of many of the leaders of the Indian Christian community for a comprehensive church organization adapted to the country. While the community as a whole, as might be expected from its origin and history, cannot be said to have shown any strong and widespread desire in this direction, neither can it be said that there is anything within the community itself which would militate against the realization of such an ideal. This Conference, therefore, considers that every facility should be afforded for the spread and development of this desire in the Indian community at large. While this Conference believes that the Indian Church should continue to receive and absorb every good influence which the Church of the West may impart to it, it also believes that in respect of forms and organization the Indian Church should have entire freedom to develop on such lines as will conduce to the most natural expression of the spiritual instincts of Indian Christians."

At each of the local conferences in India steps were taken for the organization of provincial Federal Councils, and at the National Conference it was recommended that there be formed a National Missionary Council of India, the objects of which were declared to be: (a) To co-operate with the provincial Councils in the carrying out of their objects;

(b) to be in communication with the Continuation Committee of the Edinburgh Missionary Conference regarding such matters as require consideration or action from the point of view of the Indian mission field as a whole; (c) to take into consideration such other questions affecting the entire missionary field as may seem to it desirable; (d) to make provision for the convening of an All-India Missionary Conference when such, in the opinion of the Council, is desirable.

Everywhere in India there is manifest a desire for the more active promotion of comity and co-operation through a more strict delimitation of territory, in the transfer of mission workers, and in the treatment of persons under discipline; and by the National Conference it was declared to be desirable "that spiritual hospitality be offered to persons of whatever denomination who may find themselves in an area in which the ministrations of their own communion are not procurable." Co-operation in all forms of education was advocated in every Conference, and all Christians everywhere are urged, in the words of the National Conference, "to be instant in believing prayer to the God and Father of our Lord Jesus Christ that he will vouchsafe speedily to accomplish his gracious purpose and hasten the day when the prayer of our Redeemer may be fulfilled, and all his people be perfected into one."

The reports of the Conferences in China tell a similar story. "We recognize," declares the Canton Conference, "that the Chinese Church, both as regards her leaders and the majority of her membership, is strongly in favor of one Church, open to all Christians, and is making a more or less conscious effort to realize that aim. This does not mean that there will be a uniform statement of faith, or identity in forms of worship, or one central government, but that there will be an attempt to make this a truly Christian Church, which in all its constituent parts will comprehend the whole Christian life of the nation. . . . Our faith is in the guiding of the Holy Spirit, who will safeguard the essential liberty of the constituent parts of the Church. He, too, will enable us to share as a common possession the benefits of those varied attainments in truth, faith, and practice which each denomination holds as a sacred trust received by the grace of our one Lord. While, however, the Chinese Church should continue to receive and absorb every good influence which the Church of the West can impart, it should, in respect of forms and organization, have entire freedom to develop in accord with the most natural expression and largest cultivation of the spiritual instincts of Chinese Christians." The Shanghai Conference declared: "We can set before the Church in China no lower ideal than that of a manifest and organic unity. It should include all those within the Chinese nation who hold the truth of our Lord Jesus Christ. But this unity must be a result of spiritual growth rather than of outward organization. Organization should be expressive of the growth in unity of life."

There seems to have been general agreement in all the Conferences that the first step toward the organic unity desired is the federation of existing churches for mutual counsel and co-operation. "The differences which now characterize us," said the Shanghai Conference, "are not the results of wilful disobedience, and will doubtless disappear as we, by united counsel and work, understand each other better and attain to a fuller conformity to the mind of Christ. We believe that the way to unity will open as we patiently study the Scriptures, the past history of the Church, and the living experiences of the various present sections of the Church." The Conferences at Tsinan-fu, Peking, and Hankow expressed their convictions in practically identical terms. A National Conference on Faith and Order, a central Business Agency for all China, Boards of Arbitration for all China, fuller co-operation in all educational enterprises are among the plans suggested for the correlation of all the forces in China engaged in missionary work, while from every one goes forth an earnest call for united intercession that the prayer

of the Lord for the unity of his Church may be fulfilled.

Finally, the purpose of the Christians in China
is summed up in the findings of the China National
Conference at Shanghai in words whose significance
can hardly be overestimated: "In order to do all
that is possible to manifest the unity which already
exists among all faithful Christians in China, and to
present ourselves in the face of the great mass of
Chinese non-Christian people as one brotherhood
with one common name, this Conference suggests
as the most suitable name for this purpose. . . .
'The Christian Church in China.'"   The Conference
proceeds to recommend as steps toward a larger
unity, the uniting of churches of similar ecclesiastical
order; the organic union of churches which already
enjoy intercommunion; federation, local and provincial, of all churches willing to co-operate in the
extension of the kingdom of God; the formation of
a National Council of the Churches; the fresh study
by all Christians of the faith and order of those who
differ from them, and intercession for the increase
of the spirit of unity.

The Seoul Conference, conducted by the continuation Committee, recounts with gratitude the progress
that has been made during the last decade in unify-
ing and federating the work of the missions and
churches in Korea: "The union hymn-book; a

common name as applicable to most of the churches; the formation of a Federal Council of Evangelical Missions, and of an Educational Federation; union in the Severance Hospital Medical School, and in other educational institutions; co-operation in the Tract Society, the Bible Committee, and in other forms of work; the division of territory arranged among six of the principal missions and corresponding churches; the union of the work of four Presbyterian Missions into one Presbyterian Church; and the federation of the two Methodist missions, show that much has been accomplished." The belief is expressed that "all look forward to a closer degree of formal organization, whatever be the means through which the Spirit of God may lead."

Japan is not so far advanced in the direction of organic unity as are China and Korea; nor is the desire for a national church that shall include Christians of every name as evident as in India. "The tendency of Christianity in Japan at present," declared the Japan National Conference, "is toward the maintenance of separate churches, in their organization patterned after those in the West; but for the purpose of co-operation in work of common interest an organization has been formed which is known as the Federation of Churches in Japan. The Federation is composed of churches comprising four-fifths of the Protestant Christians in Japan, and there are indications that the churches comprising the remaining one-fifth may enter the organization in the near future." "It is the sincere hope and earnest prayer of every Christian man and woman," it was stated by the Tokio Conference, "that all the churches representing Christianity in Japan may come together and be made one in Christ, with one faith, one order, and one work; but we think it will be some time before this high ideal can be realized."

It is in part, perhaps, because in China such great distances separate the mission stations from one another, that federation there has been upon interdenominational rather than upon denominational lines, whereas in Japan the reverse has been the case; but it is evident that the sense of national unity that is spreading so widely, and impressing itself so deeply among all the peoples of the East, is making more definitely year by year, even in Japan, for a national Church that shall clearly set forth to the world the essential unity of all believers in Christ. That the problem of Christian unity is not so burning a question, as yet, in Africa arises from the lack of a common consciousness, such as is found in the East, among the scattered tribes of that great continent.

Already upon the mission fields, in individual instances, further advance toward the ideal of a united Church has been made than can be found anywhere among Western nations. The West China Missions Advisory Board, which publishes two monthlies, one in English and one in Chinese, has achieved actual union in certain educational enterprises, notably in a most successful union Middle School in Cheng-tu; and is definitely working toward the ideal of one Protestant Christian Church in West China, with a single declaration of faith as a common basis for church membership. Federation Councils are already organized and at work in at least 12 of the 18 provinces of China. In the Philippine Islands the Evangelical Union, organized in 1901 for the purpose of securing comity and efficiency, has abundantly justified its existence, and the territory has been divided among the various societies working there, who are laboring together harmoniously toward a closer and more effective affiliation.[1] A large proportion of the missionary field has been now divided by agreement between the missionary agencies into similar spheres of influence and responsibility.

The remarkable intellectual awakening which the Orient is experiencing has emphasized the necessity for schools and colleges larger in number and in capacity, and of a higher grade than individual communions are able to furnish. Both economy and efficiency are demanding that denominational agen-

[1] For further examples see the Report of the Committee on Foreign Missions of the Federal Council, December, 1912, and Dr. A. J. Brown, *Unity and Missions*, Chapters X. and XI.

cies shall unite in the establishment and support of secondary schools in the larger centers; and if the Christian college and university are not to relinquish the primacy which they have enjoyed hitherto, and to be surpassed in scholarship and equipment by the non-Christian institutions that are rising on every hand, denominations must combine their educational resources. In Peking the Methodist, Presbyterian, and English and American Congregational Boards are uniting in the development of a single university scheme with one union institution of each academic type.[1] With a similar statesmanship union universities are being developed in Tsinan-fu, Nanking, and Cheng-tu in China, and in strategic centers in other Asiatic lands. In China alone there are already about 30 educational institutions under interdenominational control.

More difficult are the problems attending theological education. In the home land theological seminaries of an interdenominational character are, for obvious reasons, exceedingly rare. On the foreign field, however, co-operation in even this form of education is being found practicable. Dr. A. J. Brown reports that "there are interdenominational theological seminaries or training-schools for Christian workers in Manila (Methodist and Presbyterian), Seoul (Northern and Southern Methodist;

[1] Dr. A. J. Brown, *Unity and Missions*, p. 159.

Northern, Southern, Australian, and Canadian Presbyterian), Peking (English and American Congregational, and American Presbyterian), Nanking (Northern and Southern Methodist, Northern and Southern Presbyterian, and Disciples), Shan-tung (English Baptist, and American Presbyterian), Bangalore (United Free Church of Scotland, Reformed Presbyterian Church of America, London Missionary Society, American Board, and Wesleyan Missionary Society), and Canton (English and American Congregationalists; American, Canadian, and New Zealand Presbyterians; English Wesleyans, and United Brethren). In Australia, the Moravians and the Presbyterians have agreed on a plan by which the former train missionaries for the mission to the aborigines of North Queensland, and the latter control and support them." "The experiment of union theological instruction," declares Dr. Brown, "begun about a dozen years ago, not without misgivings, has proved to be a signal success, and no difficulties whatever have emerged that are worth mentioning in comparison with the benefits that have accrued. Foreign missionaries have demonstrated that union in theological instruction is entirely practicable."[1]

In the field of medical education, co-operation between denominations is more easily secured. There

[1] *Id.*

are no diseases, not even spiritual diseases, peculiar
to particular denominations. Sanitation and hygiene are the handmaids of the most diverse theologies, and in the sick-room or by the bedside of the
dying, "distinctive principles" are out of place. In
China, in particular, union medical schools and hospitals are multiplying. The largest and most widely
known of these is the Union Medical College in
Peking, in which the London Missionary Society,
the American Presbyterian Mission, the American
Board, Peking University (Methodist), the London Medical Missionary Association, and the
Church of England Mission co-operate. At Hankow, Nanking, Canton, and Shan-tung similar institutions are either established or in process of organization.[1] In the Philippine Islands Baptists and
Presbyterians are uniting in the management of the
best hospital in the territory.

It is possible that this is to be the crowning contribution of Eastern Christianity to the West,—the
rich return of the Orient for the labors and treasures
expended by the churches of the Occident upon the
other side of the globe,—an example of Christian
unity such as shall provide the strongest stimulus
ever given to the unification of Christian forces at
home. Already the necessities of the foreign mis-

[1] Dr. J. B. Neal, "Union Medical Colleges in China," in *The Christian
Work*, May 22, 1915, p. 665.

sionary enterprise and the spirit of unity upon mission fields have drawn the agencies of the churches
at home into close co-operation. The greatest
obstacle to unity on the foreign field has always
been disunity among the churches at the home base.
The China National Conference, to which reference
has been made, adopted a resolution which the
churches of America would do well to heed: "Inas-
much as co-operation between the missionary bodies
working on the field is rendered almost impossible
without the sanction of the Home Boards, this Conference recommends that the China Continuation
Committee endeavor to bring about a greater measure of co-operation between the Mission Boards at
home." Thus do the children admonish their
parents!

A large measure of unity among the agencies of
the denominations at home has, however, already
been secured. For 20 years the representatives of
all foreign missionary organizations in America have
met in annual conference to consider such questions
as comity, co-operation, the forces needed for the
evangelization of the world, the division of territory,
the place of the native Church, the relations of missionaries to the native populations, and, indeed, all
questions of a common interest. Similar conferences have lately been organized in Great Britain
and Ireland and in Germany. The Laymen's

Missionary Movement, the Missionary Education
Movement, and the Missionary Volunteer Movement are all of them organizations of an interdenominational character whose object it is, not to send
out missionaries, but to foster missionary interest
and to spread missionary information throughout
all denominations.

There is no service in which Christians can engage
that can draw them together in a fellowship so strong
as does the missionary cause. Here men meet on a
level higher than their denominational divisions and
find themselves at one. Upon the platform of the
evangelization of the world all Christians can stand
together, and there they feel most keenly the bonds
that unite them. The Laymen's Missionary Movement in America has brought the men of the churches
together as no organization with a smaller or less
inspiring purpose could possibly have done. The
great Missionary Conference held in Edinburgh in
1910, the seventh of a series of such conferences,
interdenominational and international, that date
back to 1854, might well be called "Ecumenical,"
for it was the nearest approach to an all-inclusive
gathering that Protestantism has ever seen. No
other cause could have called together so representative a body. And the Continuation Committee, appointed by the Conference to carry out
the lines of work projected by it, is perhaps the

mightiest single influence in the world to-day making for co-operation and unity among the forces of
Christendom. For 13 years the Missionary Education Movement, controlled by a board chosen by
American home and foreign missionary societies in
co-operation, has been providing text-books for mission study classes and other literature of a high
order for the use of all denominations in common,
and hundreds of thousands have gained a new
knowledge of the missionary enterprise through its
activities. The necessities of the missionary cause
furnish the mightiest argument for Christian co-
operation and unity that the Church has ever faced.

Thus still another illustration is furnished of the
truth, that it is in service performed together, and
not in the discussion of their points of difference,
that Christians of every name and type are discovering how wide and deep is the measure of unity that
already exists among them, and how far-reaching are
the possibilities of a union still more real and strong.
"There has never been a time," truly says the Committee on Foreign Missions of the Federal Council,
"since the German Reformation, when various denominations were so closely engaged in co-operative
measures for promoting the kingdom of Jesus Christ
among the nations. There has never been a period
since the beginning of modern missions when denominational differences were so minimized and the

14

great fundamental truths of our blessed religion were so universally emphasized, and we advance together for the conquest of the world for Christ. More and more the united front of Christianity is presented to the united opposition of Islam and paganism, and only when this union is practically complete may one expect to achieve the victory sought."[1]

[1] *Report of the Committee on Foreign Missions at the Second Quadrennial Council*, December, 1912.

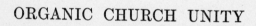

ORGANIC CHURCH UNITY

Mere federation not sufficient.—Organic unity traced through entire history of the Church.—Conditions to-day more conducive than ever to organic unity.—Experiments in actual Church union cited.—Proposed World Conference: Its origin and purpose; Relation of the Roman Catholic and Greek Orthodox Churches to the movement.—Ultimate union of all Christian forces must be preceded by unification of denominational divisions: Results already accomplished. —Union of certain denominations being attempted in many parts of the world.—Various denominational branches in America tending toward a new type of polity and worship.

CHAPTER IX

VALUABLE as has been the service rendered by the federation of the churches to the cause of the Kingdom, the conviction is steadily growing that something more is necessary if the prayer of the Lord for the unity of his disciples is to be fulfilled.

There are many Christian men, without a doubt, who have no desire for any degree of unity closer than federation can supply. They think habitually in terms of churches, never in terms of the Church. They have no expectation nor hope that the ecclesiastical fragments with which Christendom is strewn will ever be gathered into a single basket. The ideal of a catholicity one day to be visible seems to such neither possible nor desirable. To them denominationalism is not a temporary expedient, nor a recourse made necessary by the misfortunes of Christian history, but the expression of the Christian ideal; and such a federation of denominations as is exemplified in the Federal Council of Churches of Christ in America is to them the last word upon the subject of Christian unity. "There never will be a time," writes President Strong of the

University of Kansas, "when the Christian body will not be organized in different groups." "To let denominations decay," says Dr. Shailer Mathews, now President of the Federal Council, "would be to let churches decay. What we are getting now is a co-operative Protestantism. . . . I am not writing in a spirit of sectarianism, but as one who recognizes that the denominations are economically necessary to the development of a really effective Protestantism."

There are, however, many signs that the Christian consciousness of our day cannot be so easily satisfied. The process of federation has already gone too far if the churches are not to go farther. There will be an inconsistency in many of the activities in which the spirit of unity is expressing itself, as long as the imperialistic claims of the individual denominations to the exclusive possession of essential truth are unabated. The policy of interdenominational comity, reciprocal denominational exchanges of churches in over-churched communities, and the division of unoccupied territory, both at home and on the foreign mission field, into districts wherein particular denominations are invited to labor with the assurance of non-interference on the part of others, seems to be definitely accepted and established. But note what this involves. If the differences between evangelical denominations are sufficient to

make organic unity impossible without the surrender of essential truth, then they are sufficient to
make both inconsistent and wrong the concessions
that are necessary for such division of responsibility
for the vital activities of evangelism and religious
education. No denomination which sincerely believes another to be so lacking in knowledge of the
truth as to make organic unity with it impossible
has a right deliberately to commit, either in practice or in theory, the souls of any portion of the
world to the exclusive ministrations of that denomination. To do so evidently concedes that it is
what the churches hold in common that saves, and
not the distinctive principles of any one of them, and
so cuts the ground beneath denominational divisions.
The federated churches must either go forward toward organic unity, or they must retrace the steps
already taken. Dr. Newman Smyth very truly
says, "Federations of churches are to be regarded
as at best only way-stations in the progress of the
Church; the line of development of true Catholicity
runs on and on, and our denominations are called to
be through passengers. They shall not otherwise
finish their course in faith."[1]

There is to-day, it is true, as there has always
been, an invisible catholic Church, which is held
together by the mystic bonds of spiritual fellowship

[1] *Passing Protestantism and Coming Catholicism*, p. 135.

that transcend all boundaries and divisions. "Our Church," says Prof. Harnack, "is not the particular church in which we are placed, but the *societas fidei*, which has its members everywhere, even among Greeks and Romans."[1] This is a conception to which the Christian heart has clung with a persistence almost pathetic, amid all the visible disunity with which the Church has been distracted. But it is a conception that satisfies the Christian conscience less completely every passing year; and there is no indication of the spirit of our times more evident or significant than the yearning for some new and more universal order of Christianity in which the unity of the faith may be visibly manifested. It is a thought that is rising simultaneously in a multitude of minds everywhere throughout the Christian world, and that is being expressed in many ways.

The ideal of organic unity has never been completely lost from the consciousness of the Church. The Pauline ideal of the Church, that he transmitted to the local congregations he founded, was that of one body with many members, after the analogy of the human organism. "For in one Spirit," he declares, "were we all baptized into one body, whether Jews or Greeks, whether bond or free; and were all made to drink of one Spirit."[2] "Now

---

[1] *What is Christianity?* p. 276.   [2] I. Cor. 12 : 13.

ye are the body of Christ, and severally members thereof."[1] The wonderful panegyric of Christian love with which he follows the description of the organic unity of the Church is meant to extol the principle that is necessary for its attainment and maintenance. The Church, even in the period of its bitterest contentions, has not lacked for prophetic souls whose voices have been raised in the interest of unity and peace. Calvin wrote Cranmer in 1553, "I should not hesitate to cross ten seas if by this means holy communion might prevail among the members of Christ." Said George Calixtus, professor in the University of Halmstadt, in a letter to the Roman Catholic Universities of Germany, breathing a tender spirit of reconciliation, "If I may but help toward the healing of our schisms, I will shrink from no cares and night-watchings, no efforts and no dangers . . . nay, I will never spare either my life or my blood, if so be I may purchase the peace of the Church."[2] Zwingli and Melanchthon, Grotius, Leibniz and Bossuet, Richard Baxter, Milton, Wesley, Jeremy Taylor, and John Locke were all of them advocates of Christian unity, at times when a belligerent sectarianism was tearing Christians apart.

It is true that many an irenicon devised by large-

[1] I. Cor. 12 : 27.
[2] Quoted by Peter Ainslie, *The Message of the Disciples*, etc.

hearted leaders in the past has come to naught; but is this a reason why, in this generation, earnest men should cease to pray and to labor for the unification of Christendom? History presents no period so full of encouragement for the friends of a real and visible unity of the Church. We live in a new age wherein many of the barriers that once kept men apart have been broken down. Geographical hindrances have largely disappeared: we are nearer to England to-day than was New York to Boston at the beginning of the last century. Modern methods of travel and of the intercommunication of thought are fast transforming the world into a single community. In America, at least, political barriers have been overthrown, and free churches, in a free land, meet each other upon the same level, equal in all their privileges. Theological bitterness is fast disappearing and mutual respect and esteem are taking its place. The divided churches are being driven together: they are also being drawn together by the cords of love. The democratic and co-operative spirit of the times provides an atmosphere favorable to the unification of the churches, particularly in the United States, where men of so many racial strains are learning to live and labor together and to sink their differences below the level of the new patriotism that unites them. Prejudices as well as peoples are in solution in "The Melting Pot."

The utilitarian and pragmatic spirit of the prevalent philosophy, with its appetite for theories that "work," that produce results, and its regard for the practical, tends to withdraw interest from the abstractions that divide, and to concentrate it upon the activities that unite. There is less disposition to-day than ever to judge institutions by their claims: "by their fruits ye shall know them." Creeds are measured by the same criterion. Christians in the pew are willing to sacrifice for the spread of the kingdom of God, but not to perpetuate divisions in the Church unless some unquestionably valid reason for their perpetuation can be offered. It may be that the present halt in the enthusiasm of missionary propaganda may be due, not to any failure of interest in the supreme mission of the Church, but to a growing suspicion that there is something fundamentally wrong in the method that the Church is pursuing. That there are now in America 143 communions, every one of which justifies its separate existence by the claim to possess some distinctive and essential Christian truth not held by the remainder, would seem to prove, if these claims are true, that there are 142 necessary or valuable Christian principles lacking in each one of the denominational bodies, which to the ordinary mind proves too much, and reduces the whole sorry scheme to absurdity.

The experiments in organized interdenominational co-operation, which the nineteenth century inaugurated, prepared the way for those experiments in actual Church union which the twentieth century is now conducting. In 1804 was organized the British and Foreign Bible Society, followed in 1816 by the American Bible Society. In 1817 there was formed in Philadelphia "The Sunday and Adult School Union," the real beginning of the American Sunday-School Union, which took its present name in 1824. The Evangelical Alliance dates from 1846. Interdenominational movements such as the Young Men's Christian Association, the Young Women's Christian Association, and the United Society of Christian Endeavor are gifts of the last century to our own and have powerfully drawn the present generation of Christians of every name together. The famous fourfold proposals of the Protestant Episcopal Church for the unity of the Church were issued at Chicago in 1886; in 1895 the Congregational Churches of the United States issued their proposals of a similar character; in 1893 was organized the Brotherhood of Christian Unity, and in 1895 the League of Catholic Unity. These events indicate the point to which the movement had progressed at the close of the last century.

In 1905 was organized the Federal Council of Churches of Christ in America, which, while it does not advocate the principle of organic unity, is the most ambitious experiment yet attempted in inter-denominational co-operation. In 1910 the Protestant Episcopal Church appointed a Joint Commission to bring about a Conference for the consideration of questions touching Faith and Order, and in the same year the National Convention of the Disciples appointed a Commission on Christian Union, and the Congregationalists a Committee on Comity, Federation, and Unity, while by a noteworthy coincidence the Synod of the Dioceses of the Church of England in Australia and Tasmania was simultaneously appointing a committee to "watch for, and, if possible, take advantage of any opportunity which may be offered for further conference with other religious bodies with a view to a better understanding of our mutual position and the furtherance of union among Christians." Since that time Commissions of a similar nature have been appointed by the Presbyterians (North) and by the Church of England in Canada.

The Episcopal Commission on a World Conference has invited and already secured the appointment of co-operating Commissions by more than 30 Protestant bodies, among which several countries are represented. In May, 1913, a preliminary conference of members of a number of these Commissions was held in New York City, when, in a spirit of the utmost candor, with a full realization of the difficulties with which the undertaking is confronted, the first steps in preparation for the calling of such a World Conference were taken with a heartiness and unanimity full of encouragement for the future. According to the resolutions adopted at this meeting, the conception of the proposed Conference is that of "a great meeting participated in by men of all Christian churches within the scope of the call, at which there shall be consideration not only of points of difference and agreement among Christians, but of the values of the various approximations of belief characteristic of the several churches." It was further declared "that while organic unity is the ideal which all Christians should have in their thoughts and prayers, yet the business of the Commissions is not to force any particular scheme of unity, but to promote the holding of such a conference as is above described." A deputation appointed at this preliminary conference to confer with the non-Anglican communions in England, Scotland, and Ireland has since reported a favorable hearing on the part of 31 groups of Christian leaders in the countries visited, and the definite promise on the part of each that the appointment of Commissions on the World Conference would be recommended to the annual meetings of the denominations represented.

This proposed World Conference, suggested first, in Westminster Abbey, by the great-hearted missionary leader, Bishop Brent of the Philippines, adopted enthusiastically by the Protestant Episcopal Church in its General Convention in Cincinnati in 1910, and recommended by it to all the divisions of Christendom, has already received so large a measure of approval on the part of other Protestant communions, and is being projected with such breadth of view, and in so generous a spirit, that all who pray for the peace of the Church will watch, with the deepest interest and concern, the progress of the negotiations that must precede its convocation. Some have thought the literature thus far issued by the Episcopal Commission defining its character and purpose, to be too deeply tinged with sacerdotal and sacramentarian conceptions foreign to the thought of a major proportion of American Protestantism, to make it likely that such a conference could accomplish more than did the announcement of the Chicago-Lambeth Proposals of 1888. In any event, however, a frank discussion of differences and agreements upon a common platform will do much to clear the air, and to reveal the actual elements that enter into the problem of unity upon a doctrinal basis.

The plans for the Conference contemplate the participation of the Roman Catholic and Greek

Orthodox Churches, without which there can be no re-establishment of catholicity. This introduces difficulties that appear at first sight to be exceedingly great. Because of the promulgation of the dogma of papal infallibility, the possibility of reunion with the Roman Catholic Church seems more distant than at any previous time since the Reformation. "The reunion of the scattered branches of Christendom," Cardinal Gibbons has recently said, "is a consummation devoutly to be wished, and I would gladly sacrifice the remaining years of my life in lending a helping hand toward this blessed result." But he proceeds to say, "The first essential requirement is the recognition of the sovereign pontiff, who, as the successor of St. Peter, is the divinely appointed head of Christendom."[1]

It is inconceivable that Protestantism will ever so stultify itself as to give even serious consideration to such a suggestion. Yet the genius and history of the Roman Catholic Church are such that it seems to be irrevocably committed to the dogma of the infallibility of the pope, and by its solemn promulgation to have shut itself out from the possibility of change or compromise. "To feel the necessity, and to seek the ways, of gathering together the scattered members of Christ," Bishop Bonomelli of the Roman Catholic Diocese of Cre-

[1] Sept. 28, 1913, in a newspaper interview.

mona has said, ". . . is a surpassingly noble and beautiful aim, and worthy to be studied and translated into action with all zeal; and it is very consoling to see how our Protestant brothers are striving for this end with evident sincerity and thorough good-will." "I cannot, however," he continues, "shut my eyes to the very grave difficulty of the enterprise; first of all, the situation of the Roman Church, which cannot recede from its position, or yield upon any essential point of its doctrine, without being renegade to itself. The Roman Church, with its definitions, with the affirmations repeated a thousand times of its divine character, and with all the acts of its government, has cut down and is cutting down every bridge behind it. It can well allow itself to be joined by the dissident Churches with unconditional submission; but it cannot turn back, review its own decisions, modify its dogmas, change its hierarchy, lessen its authority. . . . And in this, I believe, consists the greatest obstacle to that unity, the need of which is so deeply felt."[1] But the spirit of the times is profoundly affecting this, as well as all other churches, especially in America. The powerful and wide-spread movement within the Roman Church known as modernism, which, in some of its phases, appears to be a reassertion of the primitive gospel of the apostles, and an

[1] *The Constructive Quarterly*, Sept., 1913, p. 445 ff.

15

approach to the evangelical principles held by
Protestantism, is a sign of promise of a better
understanding between these two great divisions of
the Church, even though the outcome of that
movement is still in doubt. If some day there should
sit upon St. Peter's throne a modernist pope, sus-
ceptible to the thousand influences that are empha-
sizing the simple forms of experience and belief
which characterized the life of the earliest disciples
and that are drawing Protestants into a new unity
upon the basis of a New Testament Christianity, the
hope of a closer approach of Catholic to Protestant
would receive an impetus quite beyond our present
ability to measure.

There is no apparent indication of the drawing
together of the Roman Catholic and Greek Orthodox
Churches. "It might seem," writes Archbishop
Platon of the Greek Church, "that no Church is
closer to the Orthodox than is the Roman Catholic.
Chief among their resemblances, the two have the
same number of sacraments; yet the distance between them is so great as to terrify us; it is almost
immeasurable."[1] So far as the relation between the
Greek Orthodox and Protestant communions other
than the Anglican is concerned, it is sufficient to
say that the grounds upon which Archbishop Platon
thinks some approach of Anglicans and Greek Ortho-

[1] *The Constructive Quarterly*, September, 1913, p. 434 ff.

dox Christians to one another may be possible, namely, the rejection on the part of the Anglicans of the dogmatic authority of the Thirty-nine Articles of the Church of England, which deny the sacramentarian character of holy orders, would probably raise an issue upon which most non-Anglican bodies would find it difficult to unite with either Anglicans or Greeks. Many of the obstacles that stand in the way of Church reunion must be left to time and the Spirit of God to remove, in the confidence that what to man may seem impossible, is possible to God.

The ultimate union of Protestantism with the Roman and Orthodox Churches must in any case be preceded by the reunion of Protestantism itself. To that practicable and hopeful task the advocates of Christian unity within the Protestant churches will do well for the present to confine themselves. And the first step in that direction must surely be the combination of the various divisions of particular denominations. Unity is probably to come by piecemeal. Of the 12 bodies of Presbyterians, 18 of Methodists, and 13 of Baptists, the larger branches are kept apart by the purely geographical divisions of North and South. There is no latitude nor longitude in the kingdom of God, and when these artificial divisions are swept away by the rising tide of Christian love, the way will be cleared for the union of the manifold varieties of varieties of Christians that are separated now by distinctions often so minute as to be indiscernible. When the Director of the Census can distinguish between two Christian bodies only by the difference in the color of the covers of their respective annual reports,[1] it would certainly seem that unity might be possible without loss to either. The combinations of denominational fractions into integers are taking place with increasing frequency. Already Baptists and Free Baptists have consummated a practical union in their missionary agencies, and a complete union in many of the states. The Old School and the New School Presbyterians, who divided in 1837 on doctrinal grounds, came together again in 1869 on a basis of orthodoxy and liberty, while in 1875 four divisions of Presbyterians in Canada came together in a single organization, and the following year saw the combination of the Presbyterian and the United Presbyterian Churches of England.

More recently, in 1900, the United Free Church of Scotland was formed to include the Free and the United Presbyterian Churches of that country, and almost simultaneously six Presbyterian churches in Australia and two in New Zealand came harmoniously together. The Northern and Southern divisions of the Presbyterian Church, the Reformed

[1] Carroll, *The Religious Forces of the United States*, p. xix.

Church, and the United Presbyterian Church are engaged in negotiations that appear to promise a closer union of Presbyterians within the United States in the near future. Nor are the Methodists behind in this fraternal movement. The Methodists in Canada, until 1874 divided into five independent bodies, united in a single inclusive church in 1883, and a similar union has taken place in Australia. At the present moment, the two branches of the Methodist Episcopal Church, North and South, and the Methodist Protestant Church are considering the formation of a united Methodism. Already Commissions from the United Brethren and the Methodist Protestant Church have agreed to unite, subject to the ratification of their General Conferences. Such tendencies in these three typical denominations are characteristic of the spirit of the new era within other Protestant bodies. The organic union of the Lutheran and the German Reformed Churches in Prussia, long ago consummated under a single government and administration, with liberty in the use of creeds and catechisms, was no more easily accomplished than might be a similar union among the related branches of these churches in America. The desire for such formal union is spreading among all the Lutheran bodies in this country, with the possible exception of the Missouri Synod. The plans for the union of the Old Norwegian Synod, the United Norwegian Lutherans, and the Hauge Synod are already practically complete. Many Lutherans cherish the hope that by 1917, when the four hundredth anniversary of the beginning of the Reformation is to be celebrated, it will be possible to adopt some plan of union that shall be acceptable to all the Lutheran bodies in America.

Following such unification of divisions of single denominations, we may hope for the combination of such separate communions as may most effectively and easily unite in administration and service. Already the project of the union of the Presbyterian, Methodist, and Congregational churches in Canada is hopefully advancing toward completion, under the name of "The United Church of Canada," and in its magnitude and meaning it well deserves to be characterized as "an extraordinary movement, in some respects not paralleled for several centuries." Twenty years ago the Protestant Episcopal Church and the Presbyterian Church, North, entered into negotiations looking toward union, and though the plan of union failed at that time, it was for causes that would hardly prevail to-day in either communion. From South Africa we hear of attempts of Baptists, Congregationalists, Methodists, and Presbyterians to form a closer union; and from Australia, of similar attempts on the part of

Presbyterians, Methodists, Congregationalists, and Episcopalians.

In many parts of the world fresh indications of the prevalence of the spirit that is healing the divisions of Christendom and drawing the hearts of Christians together are manifest, and so rapid is the progress of the movement that it is impossible adequately to record it. Denominations diverse in their methods of government, and that have been thought to be as wide asunder as the poles in their conceptions, are anxiously seeking a platform upon which they can unite hearts and hands in their common tasks. At a recent meeting of the Free Church Council of Great Britain, which includes all the great dissenting bodies, an enthusiastic reception was given to the proposal of the Rev. J. H. Shakespeare, that all the non-conformist churches of the country should come together under the title, "The United Free Church of Great Britain." On the foreign mission field, as we have seen, the cause of Christian unity thrives apace, and the anxiety of its best friends is lest its progress be more rapid than wise. "The Christian Church in China" bids fair to unify, before very long, all the stronger Protestant forces of the republic, and the spirit of China is reflected in all Oriental missionary situations. We are in the midst to-day of a mighty movement, as significant as the Reformation, that is sweeping

with irresistible power over the entire world, and
that is shortly to change the face of Christendom.
Who can doubt that it is of God?

The churches in America are learning and borrow-
ing from each other, and approximating to one
another in many respects. The tendency upon the
foreign mission field to-day is toward as large a
measure as possible of independence and self-govern-
ment for the local church. In America, even in denominations episcopally governed, there is a larger
degree of independence of action upon the part of
the local congregation than would have been possible
a quarter of a century ago; while, on the other hand,
there is a decided tendency toward co-ordination
and centralization among denominations of the
congregational and independent order. The observance of the church year is coming into increasing favor among communions that once wholly
ignored it, and liturgical embellishments of the
service are finding their way into non-liturgical
churches. Many indications point toward the development of a type of church to which no denomination at present wholly conforms, but to
which every denomination is contributing something distinctively its own.

The establishment of the *Constructive Quarterly*,
in 1913, a magazine of the highest order, whose
avowed purpose it is to create "a better understand-

ing between the isolated communions of Christendom," is at once a sign of the spirit of the times, and likely to become a powerful influence in accelerating the spread of that spirit. "It is not neutral territory that is sought," declares the publisher, "where courtesy and diplomacy would naturally tend to avoid issues and to round off the sharp edges of truth and conviction, but rather common ground where loyalty to Christ and to convictions about him and his Church will be secure from the tendency to mere compromise or to superficial and artificial comprehension. The purpose is to create an atmosphere of mutual confidence and to induce a better understanding and a truer sense of fellowship."

If this movement is of God, nothing can check it, and he who would serve his generation must lend his hand to further it. "The reunion of Christendom," declared Prof. Goldwin Smith, "is likely at last to become a practical aim. Probably it would be a greater service to humanity, on philosophical as well as religious grounds, to contribute the smallest unit toward this consummation, than to construct the most perfect demonstration of the free personality of man. As things are, rationalism and fatalistic reveries may be laboriously confuted, but amidst the energies and aspirations of a regenerated Christendom they would spontaneously disappear."[1]

[1] *Lectures on the Study of History*, p. 181.

Questions as to procedure and method are still in solution; but this great guiding principle, at least, is emerging from the aspiration, and prayer, and free discussion which are gathering about the great theme, that unity will manifest itself in proportion as the hearts of Christian people are prepared for it, and as the tide of devotion to the Head of the Church, and to the cause of his Kingdom rises to the flood.

"I stood beside the sea one day,
        The tide was low;
        With quiet flow
It scarcely lapped the ocean's rim,
Whose waving lines, now clear, now dim,
Revealed the shelving, sandy beach,
        Where oft the waves
        To watery graves
In quick succession swiftly bore
Each other as they climbed the shore.
The little hollows in the sand,
        Like silvery nests
        Where sunshine rests,
Just for the time appeared to me
As lasting as the shore to be;
But later, when the tide had turned,
        I found no trace
        In any place
Of all the basins, which had seemed
So lasting as they gleamed
Beneath the glowing summer sun.
        Why had they fled
        Like bright hopes dead?

Because the ocean in its sweep
Had gathered all in one great deep.
Here in the pools upon the sand
    I seem to find
    Within my mind
A type of churches, sects and creeds,
Established for the great world's needs;
Just for a while they will remain,
    Each with its plan
    For blessing man,
Till God's great love, like ocean-tide,
In one shall all divisions hide.
Then, folded on our Father's breast,
    Like tired child
    That wept and smiled,
At last, we all shall come to see
One Church, in its divinity."[1]

[1] Margaret May, "Pools in the Sand."

THE BASIS OF ORGANIC UNITY

True basis of organic unity.—Other foundations discussed; The Anglican ideal; Proposals presented by the General Convention of the Protestant Episcopal Church.—The two theories of the Christian ministry, the sacerdotal and the Protestant, stated.—Difference of opinion among Anglican scholars concerning apostolic succession.—Unity not to be found in agreement concerning validity of ministerial orders. —Lord's Supper and baptism cause of differences.—Uniformity in practice and doctrine concerning the ordinances not essential to organic unity.—Unity not to be secured by absorption.—Ancient creeds or decrees of Councils do not offer a basis for organic unity.—Unity in the apostolic Church among men of different temperaments and convictions.— Love for Christ and for one another secret of past and future organic unity.

CHAPTER X

THE BASIS OF ORGANIC UNITY

THE only basis upon which the organic unity of all denominations in a single church can ever be secured and maintained is that upon which the unity of the first disciples rested,—loyalty to God in Christ and a personal experience of his presence and power within the individual soul. Back to the first century we must go, to the living springs at which the earliest Christians drank, if we are to find that source of fellowship in service and worship of which the Lord of the Church was thinking when he prayed "that they may all be one; even as thou, Father, art in me, and I in thee, that they also may be in us."

Other foundations have been and are still proposed as those upon which the unification of Christendom should be attempted, particularly identity of church polity, and of creed; but in no one of them is there any promise of success. The tenacity with which the divided churches cling to conscientious convictions as to doctrine, and to cherished modes of worship or forms of polity that they believe to be authoritative, is neither to be ignored nor deprecated. The lessening of the force of religious conviction would be too high a price to pay for unity, greatly as that is to be desired, since fidelity to conscience is to be preferred above it.   The only unity for which the Church can pray is one that leaves these intact and free to develop in all their diversity; for even the divisions within the ranks of the Church are not so threatening as would be the deadening effects of uniformity.   It is not necessary, however, that forms of polity shall be identical before the Church can be united; or that rituals, helpful to the spirit of worship of any body of Christians, shall be discarded;   or that doctrines conscientiously held shall be abandoned.   The level of attachment must be deeper than any one of these, and sought in the possession of a common spiritual experience which is essential, as these are not.   "In essentials unity, in non-essentials liberty, and in all things charity" is the only possible program by which the unification of Christendom can be secured.

The divided churches can never be frozen together: they must be welded into one if the union is to be either strong or permanent.   That neither polity nor doctrine will suffice for a basis of the reunion that Christendom is seeking is evident from the history of the attempts to secure it upon such foundations.   Neither the Roman ideal of formal unity under the absolute authority of the pope and the Roman *curia*, nor what may be called the Greek ideal, based upon a rigid orthodoxy, goes deep enough to serve as the foundation of a unity that shall be spiritual and vital. The Anglican ideal combines both of these elements, being that of organic and visible unity on a fourfold basis: the Scriptures, the two ancient creeds, the two great sacraments, and the historic episcopate; but it is questionable whether it contains any larger promise of success than those which have preceded it.

This last proposal, the most famous ever propounded for the unity of the Church, attracted at its appearance the attention of the entire Christian world. It has been the rare privilege and honor of one of the smallest Protestant bodies in America to be the first to make definite overtures to the divided Christian forces, and even to be followed by the mother Church of England. These propositions, first issued in 1886, by the General Convention of the Protestant Episcopal Church in Chicago, and, in 1888, reissued, with minor changes, by the Conference of Bishops of the Anglican Communion, held in Lambeth Palace, read as follows:

That, in the opinion of this Conference, the following Articles supply a basis on which approach may be by God's blessing made toward Home Reunion:

(a) The Holy Scriptures of the Old and New Testaments, as "containing all things necessary to salvation," and as being the rule and ultimate standard of Faith.

16

(b) The Apostles' Creed, as the baptismal symbol; and the Nicene Creed, as the sufficient statement of the Christian Faith.

(c) The two Sacraments ordained by Christ himself,—Baptism and the Supper of the Lord,—administered with unfailing use of Christ's words of institution, and of the elements ordained by him.

(d) The Historic Episcopate, locally adapted in the methods of its administration to the varying needs of the nations and peoples called of God into the unity of his Church.

These proposals, which have called forth volumes of comment and criticism, have performed a most valuable service in bringing forcibly to the attention of the Christian world the question of unity and the elements that are involved in it. The first three propositions have received wide acceptance on the part of representatives of evangelical denominations; the center about which controversy and dissent has gathered being the fourth, which deals with the historic episcopate. If this proposition is concerned merely with a form of church polity, the strength and fervor of the dissent and opposition which it has aroused would seem to be disproportionate to its importance. The episcopate presented as an historic institution apart from any theory of its origin and claims,—that is to say, a mere governmental as distinguished from a sacerdotal episcopacy,—would probably not be repugnant to other Protestants. If the Church were forced to choose between the two, it would doubtless prefer hierarchy to anarchy. Episcopacy is already the *de facto* government of three-fourths, if not of four-fifths, of Christendom. Of the three prevalent forms of polity, congregational, presbyterial, and episcopal, however, scholars appear to agree that all co-existed, in germ at least, in the undivided Church of apostolic times. No one of them seems to have so far established its pre-eminent efficiency as to have proved itself to be fittest of all to survive and to control the Church of the future. Questions of polity, therefore, should not be permitted permanently to divide the Church.

Much cannot, however, be expected for the cause of unity from agreement in polity alone. The several episcopally governed denominations, or congregationally governed denominations, are no nearer to each other than are episcopal to congregational bodies. Polities will not serve as a ground of unity, though they may, if associated with theories of their exclusive validity, prove to be a ground of division.

It is because of the persistent suspicion that "the historic episcopate" as here suggested is associated with such a theory that the Lambeth Proposals have not received a wider acceptance on the part of non-Anglican churches. It is not to the historic episcopate, but to the dogma of an "apostolic succession" usually attached to it, which makes the Church dependent upon a valid administration of the sacraments, and this in turn dependent upon a sacerdotal theory of the ministry, that the great mass of Protestantism objects. There are two theories of the Christian ministry that are diametrically opposed to one another. One is based upon the conception that "the Validity of Orders depends upon the Apostolic Commission perpetuated in unbroken succession of the ministry in the Christian Church."[1] Those who hold it declare "that our Lord commissioned the Twelve with his authority over his Kingdom or Church, and that this authority was to be exercised in the use of the functions of prophecy, priesthood, and royalty, reflecting his own authority in these three spheres. They had (1) prophetic authority to preach and to teach; (2) priestly authority to celebrate the sacraments of baptism and of the Lord's Supper and conduct the worship of the Church; (3) royal authority to organize the Church, and to govern and discipline the disciples whom they received into the Church by baptism and whom they retained in the fellowship of the Holy Communion. In the first of these commissions the prophetic authority is most prominent, in the second the power of the keys, in the third the priestly or sacramental function. But they all are involved in

[1] Prof. C. A. Briggs, *Church Unity*, p. 103.

the true functions and full commission of the apostolate and their successors in the Christian ministry. . . . Jesus Christ . . . committed his authority while absent from this earth to a ministering body which should exercise all these functions on his behalf and for the benefit of the entire Kingdom."

Quite irreconcilable with such a theory is that usually held by evangelical Protestant churches, namely, that all spiritual authority is resident in personality, and is dependent upon spiritual qualifications, and, by its very nature, cannot be conveyed from those who have it to those who have it not. Spiritual grace, according to this conception, cannot be transferred like a package over a counter; nor transmitted cutaneously, as it were, or by physical contact, as electricity from a Leyden jar. He who would possess and exercise it must gain it directly at its source, from the great Head of the Church. All that the Church can do is to recognize these qualifications where they exist, and set its seal upon them. No compromise is possible between the two theories of the Christian ministry, the sacerdotal or priestly, and the republican or Protestant: they represent two mutually contradictory conceptions of religion. To many the idea of the transmission of authority in religion within a priestly hierarchy seems to belong with the monarchical scheme of government, the theory of the divine right of

kings, and the succession of kings within a single
dynasty, which were the prevailing notions in the
formative years of the Church, and which so profoundly influenced its thought and development;
but it appears to such to be out of place in an
era of democracy, when all men are proclaimed to
be equal in political rights and in the sight of God,
and under a republican form of government where
all authority is delegated by the people to those
believed to be morally and spiritually competent
to wield it. In a republic the son no longer succeeds his father in places of authority, nor does the
incumbent nominate or appoint his successor in
political office. The atmosphere generated by republican institutions is inhospitable to the dogma of
an apostolic succession: it finds no analogies in other
fields, and speaks in a language which experience can
no longer interpret.

The whole contention, moreover, seems to a large
section of Protestantism to be quite foreign to the
real purpose of the Church. The Apostle Paul declares that he might have prided himself upon
ecclesiastical regularity. He tells us that he was
circumcised the eighth day, a Hebrew of the He-
brews, as touching the law, a Pharisee,—but that he
counted all this to be loss for Christ. Such claims
had their value, and such qualifications their potency,
under the old régime of the law; but under grace

they were worthless. Christianity, as Canon Fremantle of the Anglican Church has forcibly pointed out,[1] is, according to the New Testament, primarily a life, and only secondarily a system of doctrine, public worship, and clerical government. "Why, then," he asks, "is so disproportionate an amount of Christian effort spent on these last? And why are disputes about them allowed to hinder us from any serious and united movement for making the common life really Christian?" It must be acknowledged that union with Christ constitutes a Christian, and that all who are accepted of Christ are members of his Church, in whatever communion they may be found, and it would not appear that such membership can be made to depend upon grace conferred through any human channels whatsoever.

As to questions of historic fact upon which the doctrine of an apostolic succession depends, there appear to be grave differences of opinion among scholars of the Anglican communion, and it is little wonder that the remainder of American Protestantism is unwilling to accept the doctrine as an essential part of the program of Christian unity until Bishops Gore and Hall and Professor Moberly, who profess it, can be reconciled with Bishops Lightfoot and Brown, and Professor Hort, who reject it. For

[1] *The World as the Subject of Redemption*, p. x.

many Protestant bodies the ground is cut below all such controversies by their conviction that even if the facts in question were substantiated, and the theory justified, no spiritual gain would accrue to the Church, or any *jure divino* authority be established. They ask only for the marks of fidelity and efficiency in Christian service, and count these to be adequate credentials for the exercise of a Christian ministry.

It is safe to say that the prevalent spirit of Protestantism as a whole offers no hope that a basis of agreement and unity will ever be found in a common doctrine as to what constitutes a valid order of the ministry of the Church. The Roman Catholic Church admits the validity of the orders of the Greek Orthodox Church, yet no two churches are farther apart in their sympathies. Both the Roman and the Greek Churches, on the other hand, deny the validity of the orders of the Anglican and Protestant Episcopal Churches, who, in turn, deny the validity of the orders of all dissenting churches, while within the Anglican and Protestant Episcopal Churches are those who claim validity for their own orders on the ground of apostolic succession, those who doubt or deny it, and those who do not regard apostolic succession as essential to such validity. Evidently there is no way out of our disunity in this direction. Moreover, it does not seem likely that unity will ever be achieved by any method which, by requiring re-ordination, or otherwise, discredits the credentials of any church or ministry that Christ has honored with his presence and blessing, and denies its right to labor in the Lord's vineyard. Opinions as to the validity of orders are among the non-essentials with regard to which the widest liberty must be allowed. In the coming catholicism there must be made room for the hospitable reception of the most diverse conceptions as to ecclesiastical regularity.

It is one of the sad effects of the divided state of the Church that Christian institutions that were originally meant to manifest the unity of the Church often serve to accentuate and widen the gulfs that separate one Christian body from another. This is true of the sacraments, which, variously conceived and administered, have become the occasion of division. It is at the Supper of the Lord, significantly called the "holy communion," where Christians partake of the one body broken for all, that they divide to right and left. There is a pathetic note in the statement adopted by the Lahore Conference of workers of all denominations in India, called by the Edinburgh Continuation Committee, in which this gathering of Christian men and women, eager for a larger manifestation of the spirit of unity, after declaring that "it has to be recognized, with whatever regret, that we belong to various branches of the Church of Christ which on certain questions of order and polity hold divergent views," proceeds to resolve that "it is, for the present, advisable for us to refrain from considering that the absence of the observance of the Sacrament of the Holy Communion at interdenominational gatherings implies a lack of the spirit of unity." Thus, too, Christians, though "in one Spirit all baptized into one body," are divided by questions as to the mode and subjects of the ordinance of baptism. "On the question of requirements for baptism," declared the Lahore Conference, "we recommend that, owing to the wide diversity of practice in our Missionary Societies, a serious attempt be made to have greater uniformity of conditions required of candidates for baptism." This is a consummation devoutly to be wished also in the home land.

Agreement in doctrine and practice with respect to the sacraments is, nevertheless, not sufficient to effect the unity of the Church, nor ought differences of conception here to be sufficient to prevent it. The Roman Catholic and Greek Churches agree on such points also, but this does not bridge the chasm that separates them. Baptists and the Disciples of Christ are in accord in the practice of immersion, but it has not drawn them together a whit. On the other hand, it is possible for those holding widely divergent views as to the meaning, mode, and efficacy of the sacraments, to unite in worship and service and Christian fellowship, so long as liberty is accorded to all. How shall we treat those who differ from ourselves in their interpretations of the ordinances? Just as God treats them. Does he discriminate in favor of immersionists, or bless those who hold one conception of the Lord's Supper above those who hold another? The confines of his Kingdom are broad enough to include them all.

Much the same may be said of theological formula. Creeds and confessions of faith, meant to draw Christians together, have driven them apart. Church unity never has existed, and never can be secured upon a basis of theology; but neither should controversies in this regard be permitted to keep Christian hands and hearts apart. The differences between the manifold creeds of Christendom are so extreme that it would be impossible for all Christians to unite in any formal statement of faith except in a few general and soulless propositions of natural theology. But where theology divides, religion, the life which theology often vainly seeks to describe, unites. Men may enjoy experiences essentially the same while differing widely in their interpretations of them. The centrifugal forces that drive the disciples of Jesus apart are of the head: the centripetal forces that draw them to-

gether and toward the central Christ issue from the
heart. We may expect a larger degree of agreement in doctrine after the churches have come together to pray and praise and serve than will ever
be possible before. "The time will come," it has
been well said, "when the more we differ, the better
we shall be agreed: differing in the smaller, agree-
ing in the larger things: far apart in the spreading
branches, knit together in the sturdy trunk." It is
possible now as never before to tolerate great diver-
sities of doctrine within a single Church, because
men are learning to grant to others the liberty which
they claim for themselves, to respect differences of
conviction, and to work together in spite of them.

No single denomination now in existence is fitted
to gather into itself the various divisions of Christendom and thus become that Church of the future for
which we are looking. The spirit that claims that
any single communion is entitled to be recognized
as the true Church of Christ in an exclusive sense is
hostile to the spirit of unity. The problem of unity
is not to be solved by all Christians eventually becoming Baptists, Methodists, or Episcopalians, or
by any similar transformation; nor by all Christians becoming Protestants, or all Roman Catholics,
or members of the Greek Orthodox Church. So far
as its formal organization is concerned, it is evident
that organic union must come, not through exclusion

or compromise or absorption, or by any process, so to speak, of deglutition, by which any single denomination will swallow up the rest, like another Aaron's rod turned serpent, but by comprehension. The three hundred bishops of the Anglican Church in their last conference in Lambeth Palace said, "We have set before us the Church of Christ as he would have it, one Spirit and one Body, enriched with all those elements of divine truth which the separated communities of Christians now emphasize separately. . . . We must fix our eyes on the Church of the future, which is to be adorned with *all* the precious things, both theirs and ours. We must constantly desire not compromise, but comprehension; not uniformity, but unity." These are truly irenic words. There must be abundant room within the new catholicity for differences in polity, creed, and ritual: each company of Christians must be permitted to bring into it the things that they hold sacred. Within the universal Church, which is Christ's body, there is unity amid diversity,—difference in functions and methods with unity in aim, diversity in gifts, variety in manifestations, but the one Spirit everywhere,—and the whole is controlled by the Head, which is Christ. The divisions that Paul decries are those that grow out of a partisan spirit, and that rally about disruptive and partial interpretations of truth, or that cleave to human leadership, and so divide the indwelling Christ: he does not demand uniformity among the elements that compose the Church. Within the united Church of the apostles there was abundant opportunity for differences of view and of activity. Paul and Peter did not always see eye to eye, but both frowned upon the spirit of faction and dwelt together within a catholic Church.

Where, then, shall we find a foundation broad and stable enough for the erection of such a Christian edifice as this? Shall we seek it by returning to the days that preceded the Reformation and starting anew? "The only way in which Roman Christianity and Protestant Christianity can legally combine," writes Prof. C. A. Briggs, "is for Protestant Christianity to frankly recognize the technical irregularity of the Reformation; its revolutionary and illegal character; and for the Roman Church to repeal and recall all its unrighteous discipline."[1] History cannot be thus unwritten. The consequences of the Reformation are irrevocable, and are too precious still in the eyes of those who have profited by them to be regretted or revoked. Nothing that this generation can do could reach back into the past and stay the hands that lighted the fires of Smithfield, Prague, and Rome, any more than it can dim the luster of the names of those who died amid

[1] *Church Unity*, p. 174.

their flames. And even if Protestantism could be so recreant to its trust and so false to its history, and to the prophets and martyrs whose deeds adorn its annals, as to desire to undo the past, could Roman Catholicism, now fettered by the doctrine of the infallibility of its titular head, retract its pronouncements or retrace its steps? Protestantism must first unite upon a platform so broad that all can stand upon it, and then a united Protestantism must meet a united Catholicism upon the level of equality. There is no hope for organic unity except upon what Bishop Brown of the Protestant Episcopal Church has called the "level plan."

No progress can be made by seeking a basis of reunion in the days before the Reformation, or in going back to the fifteenth century to begin over again. Nor shall we succeed better if we go still further back to the second and third centuries, to find in the diocesan bishop (then first distinguished from the parochial bishop, elder, or presbyter), and his successors, the visible expression and source of the unity of the Church, for, as we have seen, agreement as to polities and sources of authority do not suffice to create or to sustain the unity of the Church to-day. The doctrines of these early days, moreover, will serve us no better. "The basis of union," said Dr. Döllinger, "must be the Nicene Creed, and the decisions of the first three General

Councils." But, alas, the decrees of the first three
General Councils did not secure unity of spirit in
their day, and a unity in form devoid of spiritual
unity is a body without a soul, powerless and dead.
Subscription to creeds will not unite the Church
to-day. There are churches, such as the Baptist,
without any written creeds whatsoever, that manifest
a rare degree of unity in both faith and order. Nor
is the desired end to be secured by returning to that
conception of the ordinances that was unfolded during these many years. How far doctrines as to the
efficacy of the sacraments, as they have been developed through the centuries, have been influenced
by the impact of pagan ideas upon the gospel is a
question upon which there is a legitimate difference
of opinion among historians; but this at least is
true, that questions as to polity, creed, and sacrament are all of them dependent upon questions of
historic fact, and this alone is sufficient to destroy
their usefulness as grounds of unity. Over and over
again the Church has made the mistake of pinning its
faith to statements of fact which historical criticism
may at any moment prove to be untenable. It is
impossible to build so great a structure as the unity
of the Church upon such shifting ground.

The only dependable basis for the unity of the
Church is to be found, not in the field of doctrine,
government, or ordinances, but in the field of spir-

itual experience, in a living experience of God in Christ in the heart of the believer, the same to-day as in the first days of the Church, and that is capable of perpetual reproduction in the lives of men of every age, and so of continual renewal and substantiation for each generation as it appears. Of Peter's confession of his Lordship, Jesus said, "Upon this rock I will build my Church." The basis of unity that sufficed for the first disciples is the only basis that can serve the twentieth century.

If we are to find in history the bond of unity for the Church of the future, we must go back to the beginning. To return to the days that preceded the Reformation or even to those of the Church of the first centuries will not avail; for with every development in the complexity of faith the seeds of division have been more widely sown. If a foundation is to be found that cannot be shaken, we must dig below the accretions of the centuries, beneath the loam and the subsoil of Christian history to the simple faith of the first disciples of the Lord. The fewer and simpler the principles reckoned essential, the larger the number who can stand together upon them. Particularity breeds diversity. What held together the group of disciples that met on Pentecost in the upper room? Subscription to a written creed? Christians before the creeds were more truly united than have been any

Christians since, and the cause of unity might be advanced if every historic creed outside the Bible were forgotten or lost.   Was it acceptance of a particular form of Church polity?   Their sense of unity was not the result of a polity, but their polity, when it developed, was the expression of their unity.   What then held them together?   Love for their risen Lord!   Each bound to the Christ, they were bound to one another.   Each conscious of his indwelling life, they were united in the enjoyment of a common experience.   There were differences within that little company that were most divisive: differences, of temperament, as between John and Peter; here, too, was Simon the zealot, an insurgent against the Roman government on account of the imposition of the taxes, and Matthew the publican, a collector of those taxes.   Yet in Christ they were united. It was first a union of spirit and experience, and it resulted in a formal and organic unity in work and in worship.

Mere oneness is not sufficient: it must be oneness in Christ—"as thou, Father, art in me, and I in thee; that they also may be in us."   That has been the essence of true catholicity from the beginning.   "We first meet the word catholic," says Professor Briggs, "in the epistle of Ignatius, the Bishop of Antioch, to the church at Smyrna early in the second century, in the sentence, 'Wheresoever the bishop shall appear, there let the people be; even as where Jesus may be, there is the catholic Church.' The catholic Church is the Church gathered about Jesus as its head, just as the church at Smyrna was gathered about its bishop. The catholic Church is thus the universal Church as distinguished from the local church, the Church throughout the whole world, under Jesus Christ, the bishop of all.'[1] The achievement of unity upon a basis short of this: a visible, organic unity cemented by anything other than a common loyalty to "Jesus Christ, the bishop of all," while it might seem to promise a vast increase of efficiency and power, would prove to be the undoing of the Church.

It is in this direction that Christendom must look for the basis of the unity for which it prays. Creed must be reduced to the irreducible minimum as a requirement for membership in the universal Church. Says Professor Denney in his *Jesus and the Gospel*, "The symbol of the Church's unity might be expressed thus: 'I believe in God, through Jesus Christ, his only Son, our Lord and Saviour.'" Is more than this needed? The widest liberty of conviction as to the validity of Church polities must be accorded. Said Edward Stillingfleet, Bishop of Worcester in the middle of the seventeenth century, "For the Church to require more than Christ him-

[1] *Church Unity*, p. 47.

self did, or make the condition of her communion
more than our Saviour did of discipleship, is wholly
unwarranted." Wise words, and as true as when
first spoken. To go "back to Christ" is to go forward. Folly and mistake began when the Church
forsook its Lord, and betook itself to the ordinances
of man. Disunion began when the Church over-
took its Master and sought to pass him by. But
to-day the Christ still leads his Church, and from a
position far in advance of it beckons it forward, and
calls upon it to renew its allegiance to the simplicity
of the gospel.

> "We faintly hear, we dimly see,
>   In differing phrase we pray;
> But dim or clear, we own in Thee
>   The Light, the Truth, the Way."

The Church has much to forget before it can attain unto the unity of the faith: it has also much to
remember. The sovereign cure for the evils of disunion into which Christianity has fallen is a purer
and simpler Christianity. The Christ who prayed
for the unity of his Church alone can effect it; but
he must be given the leadership of it. As mutual
love of parents and children holds the home together, in spite of differences of belief and temperament among the children, so love for one another
and for their Lord must hold together Christians

of every name, if they are ever to be held together. For this there is no substitute in schemes of Church unity, whether federal or organic. When love of the Lord which draws them together is strong enough to overcome their affection for the "petted notions, fondled theologies, and idolized ceremonials" which separate them, nothing can keep them apart: they will come together and find a way of reconciling their differences, or labor and pray in a united Church in spite of them. William Denny very truly says, "There are problems in the spiritual and social world which are like some of our metals, altogether refractory to low temperatures. They will only melt with great heat, and there is no other way of melting them." When Christians desire it earnestly enough, desire it more than they desire a hundred and one other things which are incompatible with it, desire it passionately, the lost secret of Christian unity will be discovered again, and the prayer of the Lord of the Church that his disciples may be one will be fulfilled.

INDEX

INDEX

265

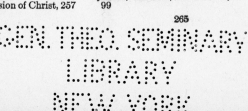